The
Coarse Fishing
Handbook

The **Coarse Fishing** Handbook

A Guide To Freshwater Angling

TONY MILES
CONSULTANT: BRUCE VAUGHAN

This edition published in the UK in 2009 by
Apple Press
7 Greenland Street
London NW1 0ND
www.apple-press.com

ISBN: 978-1-84543-295-9

This book was designed and produced by
Anness Publishing Ltd
Hermes House
88–89 Blackfriars Road
London SE1 8HA
www.annesspublishing.com

Contents

The Art of Coarse Fishing

Many people have a problem with the term "coarse fishing". It implies that there is something rather uncouth or unsophisticated about the pastime or even the anglers who pursue it. People have claimed that the term came about because trout and salmon, the main game fish, were delicacies on the table, while freshwater fish such as roach, bream and chub are coarse tasting and unpleasant to eat. Others claim it was because the best trout and salmon fishing in England was the preserve of the rich, although everyone could always fish for trout in Scotland.

Fortunately today all anglers are united in their pursuit of unpolluted rivers and ethical angling practices. There has seldom been a better time to be a coarse fisher: modern tackle is vastly improved, waters are better managed, fishing is increasingly popular and records are constantly being broken.

Introduction

The term "coarse fishing" is misleading: there is nothing coarse about this sport. Great skill and finesse are required to capture these fish. Techniques have to be refined and refined again to deceive these wily creatures. The delicacy of presentation required to tempt a crucian carp is almost indescribable; the many hours of inactivity required to catch a big bream or catfish stretches the angler's patience to the very limit. Compared with these species, trout can be easy to catch. As far as fighting ability is concerned, which is probably where the "game" of "game fishing" originated, coarse fish also compare well. Salmon fight powerfully, but pound for pound they certainly fight no harder than carp or barbel, and they fight with far less intelligence. Salmon tend to go off very strongly, but often in a straight line as far and fast as possible. Carp and barbel, on the other hand, are wilier: they are looking for that snag, the bolt hole where they can tangle the line and break free. Thankfully today, the divisions between game fishing and coarse fishing are disappearing as more anglers become all-rounders and realize that each fish has its own individual merit.

The Pleasure Angler

There are three broad sub-divisions among coarse anglers. There are those who will fish for anything that comes along. They seldom compete in matches and would never dream of sitting out all night in winter on a desolate Fenland drain in the hope of a giant zander. They are "pleasure anglers", a misnomer as all anglers get pleasure from the sport.

The Match Angler

Although not all anglers start out this way, there are those who will be drawn to the drug of competition with other anglers. They may have started by taking part in club matches and realized that rivalry with other anglers gave that extra enjoyment to their fishing. Just as there are different levels of skill and commitment to the sport among pleasure anglers, so there are among the match anglers. Some are content to remain as good club-match anglers while others aspire to the heights of competition. These are the people who have honed their skills to razor sharpness by fishing against the clock. At the very pinnacle

BELOW: **The witching hour. The angler waits as the sun sinks away in the west. Dusk and dawn are often the best times to fish.**

of the match scene there is an ever-growing body of professional anglers who consistently pit their skills against the best in the world, including men such as Tom Pickering, and triple world champions Bob Nudd and Alan Scotthorne.

The Specimen Hunter

Lastly, there are the big-fish specialists, the specimen hunters. These are the anglers who have evolved in the opposite direction to the match anglers. Rather than catch small to average fish more quickly than others, the big-fish angler deliberately slows down his or her catch rate and targets the bigger-than-average specimen. This angler will happily go hours, days, weeks or even months in the dedicated pursuit of a monster and is no longer fishing in a haphazard manner but with clear and unambiguous goals.

In the 1960s anglers realized that exchange of information was valuable, and small groups of like-minded individuals banded together to form specimen groups, in which ideas were shared. The specimen group movement advanced the pursuit of deliberately targeting big fish by perhaps decades, in just a few years.

Nowadays, there is much information available to the angler through excellent specialist magazines and television programmes. Match anglers and top specimen hunters are frequently sponsored by tackle and bait manufacturers to promote the sport, and this has increased the profile of the sport.

The Diversity of Coarse Fishing

There should be no artificial divisions between these branches of coarse fishing for it is an incredibly diverse and complex sport. There are dozens of different techniques for catching each species, and methods vary from water to water. Specialist approaches may have to be made to cope with hot or icy weather, low water or floods, high winds or darkness.

And then there are sub-divisions in each technique. Are you going to float fish for specimen roach or average roach, or speed fish for small roach in a match? If you speed fish in a match, do you use rod and line, or a pole or a whip? If a pole is the choice, do you use a wire-stemmed or a carbon-stemmed float?

Perhaps you fish for big carp and are not sure whether you should fish on the bottom or on the top, or in the margins or at range. If you fish on the bottom do you use sweetcorn or boilies, and do you fish the boilies hard on the bottom or popped up? What about loose feeding? If a boilie is the chosen hookbait, do you feed boilies by catapult or stringer? Or do you not use boilies at all, preferring trout pellets in a PVA bag? The number of individual techniques that could be discussed runs into hundreds of permutations.

For the beginner this diversity can be confusing, but in time much will become clear. You will learn as you go along and it is a great mistake to let the technicalities put you off at the outset. Angling is the greatest of all sports. It is a huge challenge, brings you close to nature, and provides hours of happiness and enjoyment. It is a vast subject and consequently there are omissions here as there is simply not room to cover all topics in detail.

Tackle and Equipment

There is a bewildering variety of tackle, bait and equipment available, most of it of excellent quality. Where specific manufacturers have been mentioned in this book, it is only because their equipment has been used and tested at firsthand. It does not mean that other manufacturers do not market products of equal quality, and you should always seek advice from a local tackle dealer.

TOP: Trotting a swim for roach in high water in early winter. These are good conditions, and the angler may expect a good bag.

LEFT: A weed raft in a small overgrown river in high summer – a likely place for fish.

Species

Barbel *(Barbus barbus)*

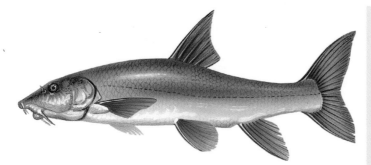

Current Record
British **17 lb 1 oz (7.739 kg)**

Season
June to March.

Distribution
Most prolific in rivers of southern England and Yorkshire.

Natural Diet
Bottom feeders taking any creatures living in the gravel.

Top Spots
River Severn, Great Ouse, Hampshire Avon and Wensum.

Top Tip
Fish with big, smelly baits in a warm winter flood, when barbel are at their fighting best.

Recognition

The streamlined torpedo shape and paddle-like coral-pink fins make the barbel one of the most easily recognizable fish in our rivers. The only fish with which it could possibly be confused is a gudgeon, and then only if it was just a couple of ounces in weight. Barbel of this size are almost never encountered by anglers, but if they are, the distinguishing features are that the barbel has a pair of barbules at the corner of the mouth and another pair on the snout. In a gudgeon, there is only a pair at the corners of the mouth. The colouring of a gudgeon is also much more mottled and generally duller.

These distinctive barbules help the barbel to locate its food, which it then sucks into a very underslung mouth which is ideally adapted for grubbing around on the river bed. Its thick, rubbery lips prevent the barbel from damaging its mouth on sharp gravel on the river bed. Strangely, for a bottom-feeding fish and one that feeds so well and effectively in low light conditions, the eyes of the barbel are fairly small in relation to body size and set high on the head. This tells us that the barbel relies more on its barbules to locate its food than it does on its eyesight. This is borne out, as one of the best times to catch barbel is at night, fishing with meat baits.

Habitat and Location

The barbel is a river fish: the modern trend of stocking these magnificent creatures in commercial stillwater fisheries, for which they are not suited, is abhorrent.

Although originally a dweller of fast, gravelly rivers, such as the River Kennet, in which they spawn most successfully and are very prolific, they also do very well in more sedate environments, such as the Great Ouse. A lower spawning success rate means that individual barbel in this type of river are becoming very big indeed.

Only a generation ago, distribution of barbel was very uneven but, as the popularity of the fish has increased, more and more rivers have been stocked, so that nowadays most parts of England and Wales have good barbel fishing close at hand.

Classic barbel swims will include beds of ranunculus, commonly called streamer weed, river bed depressions, under overhanging trees, and fast glides including the tail of weirpools. Big barbel are particularly attracted to snags, and most rivers will have swims of this sort, with a resident barbel population.

LEFT: Portrait of a big barbel showing the prominent barbules on the side of the mouth.

Size

It is very rare for small barbel to feature in anglers' catches, and the usual run of fish from all rivers would be 2–8 lb (0.91–3.62 kg). When they exceed 10 lb (4.54 kg), barbel are considered specimens and most barbel rivers now contain fish of this calibre. In the past few seasons, barbel weights have increased significantly, and where a 12 lb (5.44 kg) fish was once considered exceptional, a barbel now has to exceed 14 lb (6.35 kg) to achieve that accolade. Monster fish over 15 lb (6.80 kg) have been taken from several rivers, and the current record is a fish of 17 lb 1 oz (7.739 kg) from the Great Ouse River in 1999.

ABOVE: Playing a barbel on the River Kennet. The Kennet, the Hampshire Avon and the River Thames were traditionally the best barbel waters in the country, but many rivers not previously associated with barbel are now stocked and contain good fish. The River Severn is one of the best examples.

LEFT: The Great Ouse in summer. This water traditionally did not hold barbel as it was not a fast-flowing river, but it has recently become one of the best barbel waters and holds some very large fish.

Behaviour and Feeding Habits

Barbel are avid bottom feeders, summer and winter, although they feed very spasmodically when the water temperature falls below about 4°C (39.2°F). Much of their time is spent browsing the gravel beds, sucking out all the creatures that live there and other food items that have become entrapped. A shoal of barbel will work a gravel run in an upstream direction, and individual fish at the head of the shoal will often turn downstream with a mouthful of food before resuming station at the rear of the shoal. This behaviour is responsible for the characteristic lunging bite often associated with barbel fishing.

Barbel are easily induced to feed by anglers' baits, especially where particle baits are used in quantity.

Hempseed is well known for imparting preoccupied feeding, as are maggots, tares, worms, casters and sweetcorn. Barbel are also lovers of meaty baits such as processed meats and sausage meat.

Barbel feed well both in daylight and at night, but in clear water, in daylight, will often accept particle baits only, spooking badly on large offerings such as luncheon meat. After dark, when barbel feed entirely by smell and touch, these larger meat baits come into their own.

Warm winter floods are especially reliable conditions for producing good barbel, when the fish are actively searching for food, and mobile meat baits and lobworms are taken avidly. At this time of year, the fish are at peak condition and a good barbel is a worthy adversary for any angler.

ABOVE: Returning a 12 lb (5.44 kg) barbel to the Bristol Avon. Barbel are strong fighters and require sturdy tackle to hold them. If they are exhausted when landed hold them upright in the river, facing upstream until they have fully recovered and are ready to swim away. This principle applies to all fish.

Bream *(Abramis brama)*

Current Record
British **16 lb 9 oz (7.513 kg)**

Season
June to March in rivers, all year in stillwaters.

Distribution
Widespread in all water types except fast chalk streams.

Natural Diet
Water snails, caddis, insect larvae.

Top Spots
The Fens and Norfolk Broads.

Top Tip
Big fish are very nocturnal. Bait the swim in late afternoon and fish the dark hours for a specimen bream.

Recognition

There are two species of bream, bronze and silver; but the main one of interest to anglers is the much larger bronze bream, as silver bream (*Blicca bjoerkna*) has very limited distribution.

Young bronze bream are silvery in appearance with black fins, giving rise to confusion with silver bream, and as it is very slim and plate-like, it has attracted the nickname "skimmer" or "tin-plate bream". Over about 3 lb (1.36 kg) in weight, the colouration changes to greyish brown, although some large fish, particularly from gravel pits, live up to their name in having rich bronze hues, in some cases becoming nearly black.

As the bream grows, it changes shape and becomes deep-bodied, hump-backed and heavily coated with slime, while the markedly underslung mouth, with telescopic top lip, betrays the fact that the bream is predominantly a bottom feeder.

BELOW: **A good catch of bream taken from the River Shannon in Ireland. Bream are shoal fish and often a number can be caught from one swim. It is essential to groundbait thoroughly before starting to fish.**

RIGHT: A sluice pool on a southern country river. Although bream are not lovers of fast waters, they can be found below shallows and in slack pools on the inside of bends.

Bream has a flat-sided body that is mainly golden brown, and the pectoral and pelvic fins are tinged with red.

If you do catch a fish you think may be a silver bream, particularly in the Eastern counties of England, an easy point of recognition is that the silver bream has 44–48 scales along the lateral line while the true bronze bream has between 51–60 scales.

Habitat and Location

The bream is very widely distributed in Britain, although it is not a lover of fast-flowing rivers. Bream form vast shoals in extensive lakes such as the Norfolk Broads, in water supply reservoirs and in scenic estate lakes. They also thrive in the sedate waters of the Fens and slow-flowing rivers such as those of East Anglia, the Great Ouse and the Thames.

The biggest bream are now to be found in gravel pits, an environment that has seen bream weights increase significantly in the last 20 years.

Although rarely found in heavy flows, big bream do well in rivers such as the Hampshire Avon, where they will congregate in the deeper, slacker pools, on the inside of bends, in the steadier water below broken shallows and in any swims where fast water borders slow. In high or flood water, they are also lovers of sheltered undercuts under high banks.

Size

Bream exhibit wide size differences from water to water, and generally it is accepted that a 10 lb (4.54 kg) fish is a specimen, although many waters do not produce fish of this size. Until the advent of gravel pits, the big reservoirs produced the bigger bream, to over 12 lb (5.44 kg), but pits have now taken over this mantle.

Although some pits have shoals of average-to-big fish, up to about 13 lb (5.90 kg), it is the few waters with much lower stock density that hold the monsters. These include Queen-ford Lagoon in Oxfordshire and have produced fish up to the current record of 16 lb 9 oz (7.513 kg), taken in 1991.

RIGHT: A sluice pool on a southern country river. Although bream are not lovers of fast waters, they can be found below shallows and in slack pools on the inside of bends.

Behaviour and Feeding Habits

The natural food of bream are bottom-dwelling creatures such as water snails and caddis, as well as large quantities of insect larvae such as bloodworms. The bream's mouth is designed for vacuuming in the bottom debris to locate this food, and this activity often results in muddying of the water and the release of large mats of bubbles, a reliable guide to the presence of a bream shoal. As the fish form large shoals, they are necessarily nomadic, as they quickly exhaust the food supplies in one area. This often leads to their following well-defined feeding lines, known as patrol routes, and in some waters, particularly the meres of Cheshire and Shropshire, anglers have learned to predict the arrival of a bream shoal in a particular

area depending on the time of day. This process is helped by the bream's habit of rolling on the surface, or cutting the surface film with its large dorsal fin, just prior to feeding.

Very big bream, particularly fish in gravel pits, have the well-deserved reputation for being one of the most difficult fish to understand and catch. Even when they are located, they are often not susceptible to anglers' baits and it seems certain that for much of the time they are preoccupied by natural foods.

Although bream can be caught at all times, summer or winter, they are not lovers of very cold conditions. The bigger fish are also very nocturnal, especially in gravel pits where it can be rare to catch a bream in daylight.

Carp *(Cyprinus carpio)*

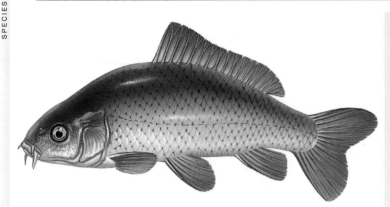

Current Records
British **56 lb 6 oz (25.571 kg)**
World **75 lb 11 oz (35.35 kg) France**

Season
June to March in rivers, all year in stillwaters.

Distribution
Widely distributed throughout Britain in all water types.

Natural Diet
Insect larvae, molluscs. Moths and flies off surface.

Top Spots
Vast number of carp lakes. Redmire and Wraysbury are both famous.

Top Tip
On big stillwaters, fish into the prevailing wind.

Recognition

The carp is the most popular sporting fish in Britain, and the largest of our cyprinids. A true wild carp, which is covered in large, regular brassy scales and has chestnut fins, is lean and muscular, often with a large tail that can give it tremendous acceleration. Although such "wildies" can reach 20 lb (9.07 kg), it is rare for wild carp to exceed 15 lb (6.80 kg).

The deeper-bodied fish, initially produced by selective breeding and which are now superseding the wild strain, grow much larger. There are many varieties that the angler may encounter: **common carp**, which are fully scaled; **mirror carp**, which are partially scaled; and **leather carp,** which are virtually without scales, except perhaps a few small ones on the shoulders and back.

Mirror carp themselves have a number of sub-varieties. True mirror carp have a few very large scales irregularly placed over the body. Much more rarely, there are mirror carp in which these scales are placed evenly along the lateral line, and these are known as linear mirrors.

Carp have four barbules, a large one in each corner of the mouth and one much smaller alongside. The long, concave dorsal fin has 20–26 rays and is totally different in shape from that of the much smaller crucian carp, which has a smaller, convex dorsal fin.

RIGHT: **Orchid Lake as night falls. Many small intimate inland lakes such as this are the home of giant carp.**

Habitat and Location

Carp is now one of the most widely distributed coarse fish, and does well in all types of water from fast-flowing rivers to stagnant pools. The most popular carp-fishing venues are stillwaters, particularly estate lakes, reservoirs and gravel pits, the latter holding the biggest fish. Favoured habitats will include overhanging marginal trees, beds of lilies, rushes or reeds, and alongside steep or undercut banks. Beds of silt which house bloodworms are also favoured, as are gravel bars in pits. The margins of

offshore islands are very reliable areas, particularly if they are overgrown. Carp are well known for following the wind on large, open waters, and in the absence of other location aids a good rule of thumb when fishing new water is always to fish into the prevailing wind.

Size

These days, most carp waters will hold plenty of fish in excess of 10 lb (4.54 kg), and a 20 lb (9.07 kg) fish is the normally accepted weight for specimen status. However, recent years have seen carp weights increase generally, so that more and more specialists regard a carp of 30 lb (13.61 kg) or even 40 lb (18.14 kg) as the target to aim for. Certainly, there are now plenty of waters holding fish of 40 lb (18.14 kg) or more, making these huge specimens a realistic ambition for the specimen hunter. The present British record is held by a fish of 56 lb 6 oz (25.571 kg) that was taken in 1998 in Wraysbury, Berkshire.

Behaviour and Feeding Habits

The natural food of carp consists of the larvae of gnats and midges, of which the bloodworm is the best known example. Carp also consume insects, molluscs and crustacea, as well as quantities of vegetation such as silkweed. In soft-bottomed lakes, the carp uses its large, extendable lips to root deep in the mud to secure its food, creating large volumes of bubbles and coloured water, a very obvious location aid for the angler.

Carp fish are also well known for browsing through marginal rush and reed beds. This causes the characteristic shaking of the plants as the carp force their large bodies through the rushes. Similarly, in soft surface weed, carp browsing underneath give rise to 'tenting', where a ridge of weed is created by the carp's back.

As well as being an avid bottom feeder, a carp also feeds off the surface, taking moths and insects as well as floating bread and is often caught on floating baits.

A surface-feeding carp is very easy to spot, as it cruises with its back partially out of the water. It is also given to rolling noisily, creating sufficient disturbance to create a flat

TOP: A slow-flowing river fringed with weed beds and bordered by willows and poplar. Carp are fond of feeding in marginal rushes on midge larvae.

ABOVE: A pristine common carp, fully scaled, about to be returned to the water.

spot in the water even when the surface is heavily broken by wind and wave action. Unless it is disturbed, a carp will feed avariciously on anglers' baits and will eat almost anything thrown at it.

Nevertheless, in spite of this happy fact, there is a great mystique about carp fishing, and carp fish are justly famous both for their cunning and great strength.

Catfish *(Silurus glanis)*

Recognition

The Wels catfish looks just like a giant
tadpole and is impossible to confuse
with any other fish. It has an
elongated muscular body, a small
rounded tail that joins the anal fin and
runs along the underside of the fish,
and a very insignificant dorsal fin. It
has a large flat head and a huge
mouth with lots of tiny, but sharp, top
and bottom teeth that feel like rough
Velcro. At the back of the mouth are
hard bony plates, used for cracking
the shells of mussels and crustacea, or
the bones of prey fish. At the top
corners of the upper jaw are two very
long feelers, or whiskers, with four
smaller appendages on the lower jaw,
used for finding food. It has highly
sensitive scent glands, making it an
efficient night feeder despite its tiny
eyes. Catfish colouration varies from
water to water: those from clear
waters can be very dark, sometimes
nearly black, and those from murkier
waters are often mid-grey or light
brown. All catfish have mottled flanks
and a creamy white belly.

Habitat and Location

The ideal catfish water is a weedy,
overgrown and very rich estate lake,
with an abundance of freely spawning
prey fish to sustain this king of
predators. Possibly the most famous
water is Claydon, Buckinghamshire
where, despite the good head of big
cats in quite a small lake, the number
of other fish is quite astonishing. The
distribution of catfish in this country
is escalating fast as the demand for
the fish grows. In most waters, in dull
conditions or at night when they are
scavenging, catfish forage quite close
to the margins. They spend bright
daylight hours under any snags in the
lake or in depressions in the lake bed.

RIGHT: **A giant among catfish. Catfish weighing over 100 lb (45.4 kg) may well exist in this country.**

Size

The present British record is 62 lb (28.12 kg) taken in 1997, but in some ways this is very misleading. There have been so many catfish waters created in recent years, stocked with imported fish, that the true potential of homegrown cats may now never be known. Stockings have been both legal and illegal. The largest catfish caught on rod and line in this country exceeded 100 lb (45.36 kg), but as this fish was stocked without the correct documentation it was discounted for record purposes. Most anglers consider a 20 lb (9.07 kg) catfish a specimen and a 30 lb (13.61 kg) fish something quite exceptional.

Behaviour and Feeding Habits

The catfish is an opportunist feeder and the ultimate scavenger. At night it roams the margins, taking swan mussels, dead fish, small mammals, frogs, newts and leeches. Even small water birds are not safe from catfish attack, and there have been several reports of baby coots and moorhens disappearing into that cavernous mouth. As well as very efficiently locating its food by its incredible senses of smell and touch, the catfish also has something else going for it. It is equipped with ultra-sensitive hearing and vibration detection, courtesy of linkage of its swim bladder to the ears via a series of small bones. This gives the cat terrific sound amplification, so that a small fish passing in pitch darkness is effectively ringing a dinner gong for a hungry catfish. Catfish anglers who travel abroad have used this sound amplification ability to their own advantage, where slapping the surface of the water with a flat paddle attracts cats from quite a distance.

Anglers have wide choices of bait, but all successful baits will have

OPPOSITE: **A very rich, shallow, estate lake. This type of water is perfect for catfish, and very large fish have been taken there.**

RIGHT: **A double-figure catfish taken from the lake at Woburn.**

either movement or a good smell. Livebaits obviously trigger the reaction to vibration but can be self-defeating if the water contains a large number of pike. Wire traces are not required for cats; in fact their very sensitive whiskers would probably reject this presentation anyway, and it is unethical to fish with this method without wire when pike are about. Obviously, this applies equally to deadbaits. Where pike are not a problem, anglers often use polystyrene balls on the hooklink to keep the bait lively, or two or three small baits on the same hook to create the effect of a shoal. The smellier the bait the better: chopped fish, squid,

fishmeal boilies, spicy sausages, liver chunks and heavily flavoured luncheon meats of a number of varieties have all caught cats.

Despite its powerful dimensions, the catfish is quite a shy biting fish, especially on hard-fished waters, and is intolerant of resistance. It is therefore important to arrange for your tackle to be free running once the bait has been taken. As many catfish waters are quite small and the fish are reliable margin feeders anyway, there is little need for long casting and freelining is a viable method. Where you need lead, say for tethering a legered livebait, make it the minimum possible.

17

Chub *(Leuciscus cephalus)*

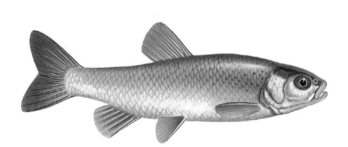

Current Record
British **8 lb 10 oz (3.912 kg)**

Season
June to March on rivers, all year on stillwaters.

Distribution
Widely distributed throughout the country, both in rivers and stillwaters.

Natural Diet
Insects, frogs, crustacea, small fish, spent moths and flies.

Top Spots
Great Ouse, Kennet, Dorset Stour, Hampshire Avon.

Top Tip
Before starting a winter chub session, walk the river and prebait several swims with mashed bread. Fish over this bait with bread flake or crust.

Recognition

The wide, black-edged scales, large mouth adorned with distinctive white lips and the big, blunt head, hence the nickname "loggerhead", make the chub one of the most instantly recognizable of all our coarse fish.

There are, however, two circumstances which make mistakes possible on the bank. The first is hybridization with other species. There have been many cases of chub/roach hybrids reported but these fish have so obviously been hybrids that all but the most inexperienced could confuse them with true chub. If you are unsure, the chub has 42–49 scales along the lateral line, and the anal fin has 7–9 branched rays, as has the dorsal.

The most common identification mistakes occur with immature chub, that can be confused with large dace. The clue here is that the anal fin of chub is convex, unlike the markedly concave anal fin of the dace.

Habitat and Location

Although primarily a river fish, the chub does very well indeed in stillwaters, especially gravel pits, where it can grow to large sizes. Big, stillwater chub have earned the reputation of being one of the most difficult specimen fish of all to tempt. Chub are very widely distributed

OPPOSITE TOP: Stalking chub in high summer. Chub respond well to the floating lure such as a fly, but are easily spooked if you approach carelessly.

BELOW: Chub can be caught all the year round. Here the angler is fishing for chub in winter and they can even be caught when there is snow on the ground.

throughout the rivers of England, Wales and Scotland, although they are not native to Ireland. They thrive in most habitats, from fast shallows to sluggish deeps, and are particularly fond of overgrown, neglected streams where they do very well and reach specimen size.

Size

The present chub record is 8 lb 10 oz (3.912 kg), taken in 1994 and is one of the coarse records under threat. The last few years have seen a dramatic increase in average chub weights, with unprecedented numbers of 5–6 lb (2.27–2.72 kg) fish reported to the angling press as well as some of 7 lb (3.18 kg). On most chub rivers, the fish will range from a few ounces to about 5 lb (2.27 kg) – most anglers would call a fish this size a specimen.

Behaviour and Feeding Habits

Chub are one of the most obliging of all fish for anglers, readily eating anything and feeding both in the hottest weather and when it is sub-zero. In summer, large natural baits such as big slugs and lobworms are taken with relish, and chub are avid feeders on crustacea such as crayfish,

ABOVE: A nice brace of summer chub caught on slugs. A fresh slug is one of the most popular baits for chub and should be collected at dawn.

small fish, particularly loach, bullheads and minnows, and any insect that might fall from the trees. They particularly love frogs and tadpoles, although these should not be used as bait as there is a general frog shortage in this country. In the evening chub are avid surface feeders, taking spent moths and flies, mayflies being a particular delicacy.

The list of anglers' baits accepted by chub is extensive, and they are as happy accepting single maggots or casters to a feeder rig as they are to

large mouthfuls of cheese paste or luncheon meat. Like barbel, chub are lovers of hempseed and a shoal of chub can be brought to a feeding frenzy over hemp and sweetcorn.

Chub are well known for their caution and are spooked very easily if approached carelessly. This explains their love for quiet, shaded places and densely overgrown stretches. During the winter, chub come to their fighting peak and generally lie in the moderate flows just out of the main push of the current. Even in winter they love a roof over their heads, and their preference for raft swims, where rubbish builds up around draping branches, is well known to all chub anglers.

Unlike roach and barbel, chub do not seem happy in the muddy water of floods and tend not to feed while these conditions persist. It is noticeable that when a chub is caught after prolonged high, dirty water, it will often be thin and anaemic looking. But they make up for their abstinence by going into a feeding binge as the colour clears and the river level begins to fall. A river fining down from a flood is one of the best times of all to be out chub fishing.

Crucian Carp *(Carassius carassius)*

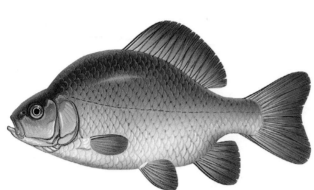

Current Record
British **4 lb 2 oz 8 drm (1.885 kg)**

Season
All year, but warmer months best.

Distribution
Patchy. Mainly found in secluded ponds and estate lakes.

Natural Diet
Shrimps, snails, insect larvae, worms and aquatic vegetation.

Top Spots
Any secluded pond that has not been artificially stocked.

Top Tip
The shyest biting of all fish. Always use the most delicate float arrangement.

Recognition

Crucian carp differ from their larger relatives in having no barbules at the corners of the mouth, a very rounded, tench-like tail and a high convex dorsal. One identifying feature is the number of scales on the lateral line: 31–33 between the upper edge of the gill opening and a point where the tail bends naturally.

Many fish claimed as specimen crucians are in fact either crucian/ common carp hybrids or brown goldfish. The problem with both of these variants is that they have no barbules, and most anglers leave it at that. However, both hybrids and brown goldfish have normal, deeply-forked carp tails and markedly long and concave dorsal fins, typical of the big carp species. Everything about the true crucian is rounded. Crucians are short, fully scaled, thickset and with tough, rubbery lips.

Habitat and Location

Crucian carp used to be very wide-spread, especially in the south. They inhabited reservoirs, estate lakes and farm ponds, but unfortunately, largely owing to the growth in popularity of carp fishing, many good crucian waters are now being destroyed because of the regularity of inter-breeding. As with the rudd, the picture is becoming blurred. True crucians are now most likely to be found in undisturbed waters; secluded woodland or farm ponds are the most

OPPOSITE TOP: An undisturbed pond in the country. This type of habitat is an ideal haunt for crucian carp and one of the few remaining locations where true crucians can be caught.

LEFT: A close-up portrait of a crucian carp showing the turned-down mouth, thick, rubbery lips and the rounded, fully scaled, golden-brown body.

BELOW: Netting a crucian carp caught in a reservoir in high summer. Crucians love to feed close to marginal cover and bankside rush beds.

obvious places. They love to feed over fine silty bottoms, close to marginal cover, and are particularly fond of bankside rush beds.

Size

The crucian carp record was vacant until recently. It reflects a ruling that all crucian records prior to July 1998 were unsafe, as the fish were almost certainly either hybrids or brown goldfish. So, a 1 lb (0.45 kg) crucian carp is a specimen and anything approaching 2 lb (0.91 kg) more than likely a hybrid or goldfish.

Behaviour and Feeding Habits

Crucian carp are shoal fish, often moving around in large numbers of mixed sizes. They feed avidly on all the food items appreciated by their larger cousins. Largely vegetarian, their food mainly consists of water plants and vegetable matter, with fresh-water shrimps, snails, blood-worms, insect larvae and worms. Crucians take in mouthfuls of mud or silt and then eject the unwanted material; this creates the characteristic bubbles and mud disturbance on the surface of the water and indicates their presence.

Unlike the larger carp, crucians do not feed much after the first frosts. As they bite delicately, even in warm weather, giving only tiny indications, a crucian bite in cold conditions, when fish are much more lethargic, would be practically undetectable.

The tackle set-up for crucians has to be very delicate to have any chance of registering their interest. They are very intolerant of resistance; even the weight of a shot on a lift float often causes them to reject the bait

LEFT: The successful angler holds a crucian carp clearly showing the rounded, fully scaled shape of the fish.

instantaneously. When crucian fishing, always plumb the float accurately to the exact depth. With a crucian bite, the angler needs to know the moment the bait has been moved, by even the tiniest fraction, and then he or she needs to strike immediately. It is a constant source of amazement that if a strike is made straight away at the tiniest of indications the crucian carp will generally be well-hooked in the back of the mouth, but if the bite is left to "develop" into a better indication, nothing happens and you wind in to find the bait gone.

For baits, maggots obviously take crucians, but a favourite bait is a single grain of corn on a size 14 super spade to 2 lb (0.91 kg) line. It pays to trickle corn grains in, perhaps a dozen every 15 minutes, plus a walnut-sized ball of groundbait to keep the fish digging. Crucian carp feed well at night and this is when you can expect better bites. Fishing for them at night with an insert waggler carrying a night light, shotted so that the merest lift or settling is immediately apparent, is the recommended method. The first two hours of darkness are generally the best, and then the hour on either side of dawn.

Dace *(Leuciscus leuciscus)*

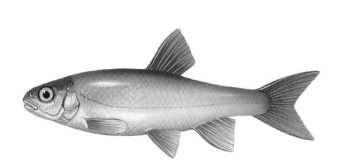

Recognition

To the inexperienced, a good dace looks for all the world like a small chub, and this has created many problems in angling history with mistaken claims for "record" dace. In overall general shape and streamlined appearance, the two fish are indeed similar in the smaller sizes, although the chub is generally a far chunkier looking character. The acid test distinguishing a dace from a small chub is the anal fin, which in dace is concave while the chub's is convex, or rounded. The overall fin colouration is also more delicate in a dace, being far paler, and varying from light orange to light brown. The head is also a giveaway. The dace looks quite demure, unlike the blunt-headed, aggressive appearance of the chub.

Habitat and Location

Dace are rarely found in stillwaters, unless these are close to river systems that have flooded. They are inhabitants of streamy sections of rivers, although the bigger fish share, with big grayling, an affinity for the deeper, steadier flows where they can be seen dimpling the surface on a summer's afternoon. They also love the fast runs through streamer weed beds on powerful rivers like the Hampshire Avon, where magnificent shoals of good dace are to be found. Where they exist, dace form large shoals that contain fish of all sizes. Dace are widely distributed throughout the rivers of England and Wales but, as with many other coarse fish, the better waters are found in the southern counties.

Size

Very few anglers can boast at having caught a dace over 1 lb (0.45 kg) in weight. There is no doubt that a 1 lb (0.45 kg) dace is an enormous fish and any fish of over 12 oz (0.34 kg) must be considered a specimen. Even at that weight, they are rare. The present record, a 1 lb 4 oz 4 dram (0.574 kg) specimen taken in 1960, is an incredible fish, and although a few ounces does not seem much, the dace record remains one of the most difficult of all angling records to crack, a challenge for the specimen hunter.

Behaviour and Feeding Habits

There is nothing complicated about the behaviour of dace. They boldly take up station in large shoals in the main flow, eagerly anticipating anything the current may bring down to them. Nothing seems to disturb their equilibrium for long, even the forays of marauding pike are forgotten quickly. Dace appear to be happy-go-lucky feeders, and it is a pleasing sight to see myriad little bars of silver twisting and turning over the gravel, as they intercept the loose-fed maggots running ahead of the trotting tackle. When there is frantic activity on the shallows from loose feed, this is the time to run a bigger bait down the closest sedate water. Some bigger

LEFT: Dace feed all the year round, and much of the best dace fishing is in winter when the fish are in peak condition. Here an angler is trotting a maggot on a south country river.

ABOVE: **A lovely catch of four dace taken trotting with a maggot.**

RIGHT: **Dace can be caught on the coldest days of the winter even when there is snow on the ground.**

BELOW: **A weir pool on the Hampshire Avon. This type of water is often the home to a shoal of giant dace.**

dace, drawn to the food in the slacker water, have been caught this way.

Dace are far from fussy eaters, and they will accept any of the normal baits used for roach and chub, in appropriately sized mouthfuls. They are particularly fond of surface feeding and take all manner of floating insect life. Fly fishing for dace is good fun, albeit frustrating. If you can connect with one in six offers on the fly from a dace you are a pretty sharp fly angler. Dace take and reject a fly like lightning. They are a good quarry in the winter, especially on a bitterly cold day, when the angler needs some active fishing to keep warm, for they share with grayling the temperament to feed with gusto in chillier weather. Do not shun their small size.

Eel *(Anguilla anguilla)*

Current Record
British **11 lb 2 oz (5.046 kg)**

Season
All year, but warmer months best.

Distribution
Widespread in all types of water.

Natural Diet
Decaying matter, frogs, fish spawn,
worms.

Top Spot
Neglected estate lakes where eels have
been left to grow undisturbed.

Top Tip
It is best to fish at night in humid,
overcast conditions. Thundery weather
is excellent for eels. Fish near to snags,
which big eels colonize in the same way
as conger eels colonize sea wrecks.

Recognition

There is only one species of eel present in British waters, the European eel, that begins its life in the Sargasso sea in the western Atlantic, before being carried to river estuaries by the warm Gulf Stream. From there eels migrate upstream as elvers, many entering stillwaters, where they may become trapped, living for many years. Most eels return to the Sargasso when they become sexually mature to spawn. This may be after about six years, although no one is certain of the exact age. Specimen eels in stillwaters are the ones of most interest to anglers. Around the world there are more than 20 families of eel.

The long, snake-like muscular body and pointed head makes the eel unmistakable, as does the dark back and creamy yellow side and belly. Adult eels possess a long narrow dorsal fin, which travels unbroken around the tail to join the anal fin, creating a very powerful rudder capable of impressive propulsion both backwards and forwards.

One very interesting evolutionary characteristic is the different mouth shape of adult eels: some are very pointed, while others are broad and flat. This suggests an adaptability depending on the diet available: the pointed-head eels possibly feed largely on invertebrates, such as worms, while the broad-headed eels feed on small fish.

Habitat and Location

Of all anglers' quarries, eels are the most nocturnal, spending much of the day resting. They are lovers of cover and will be found in holes, under tree roots and bottom snags of all descriptions. In canals, they love the darkness of bridges, and they are particularly fond of dense weed, where they will be close to a food source as the light begins to fail. A trait the freshwater eel shares with its marine cousin, the conger eel, is its liking for colonizing foreign obstructions on the river or lake bed, such as tree trunks, old cars, bicycles or shopping trolleys.

Although found in all types of water, the specialist eel angler will normally target stillwaters for the larger specimens, particularly neglected estate lakes, large reservoirs and gravel pits. The eels caught in rivers are generally of a smaller average size and very often are just a nuisance to anglers in their search for other species.

Size

Most eel specialists consider any fish over 2 lb (0.91 kg) a worthwhile capture and over 3 lb (1.36 kg) a specimen. When an eel reaches 4 lb (1.81 kg) and over, it is becoming a rare animal, and there are few anglers who can boast an eel of this size among their captures. Fish of 5 lb (2.27 kg) and over are extremely few and far between. This makes the current record of 11 lb 2 oz (5.046 kg), taken in 1978, the more remarkable, and among freshwater fish the eel surely shows the biggest discrepancy between the current record and what is considered a specimen fish. This tends to substantiate the feeling

LEFT: The head of a 6 lb (2.72 kg) eel. Eels of this size are extremely rare.

among many eel specialists that there are far larger eels in Britain than have ever been caught on rod and line. A female eel, trapped in a neglected stillwater and undisturbed by anglers, could live 25 years or more. It is therefore not inconceivable that somewhere in these islands a 20 lb (9.07 kg) eel exists.

Eels and perch have a bone under the gill cover called the operculum. It can be removed from dead fish and read like a tree trunk, as a ring is laid down each year, thus giving the age of the fish. Top eel angler, John Sidley, once killed a 6–7 lb (2.72–3.18 kg) eel to be mounted in a glass case. He had the bone read and discovered that the eel was 68 years old. He vowed never to kill another eel after that.

Behaviour and Feeding Habits

Most of the eel's feeding will be at dusk and through the dark hours, although they are often tempted out of their daytime torpor on rivers if there is a constant stream of maggots drifting downstream from an angler's swimfeeder. As darkness falls, they

TOP: A calm stretch of the Hampshire Avon where a number of big eels have been taken. The majority of large eels are caught from stillwaters where they have been left to grow undisturbed for a number of years.

ABOVE: An angler wrestling with a large eel. Eels can be very difficult to handle when caught, as they scramble up the line. Placing them on newspaper sometimes helps.

emerge from their bolt holes and begin their nocturnal patrol. Eels are very opportunistic feeders, being very catholic in their tastes, and will take all types of animal matter and pungent baits, including frogs, fish spawn, dead fish or offal, and all manner of anglers' baits.

They have a terrific sense of smell, and many modern boilies intended for carp have become much appreciated by eels, greatly to the disgust of carp anglers. They also love maggots, and fishing for other species can become impossible if a carpet of eels moves in.

A big eel will often only feed close to its bolt hole, and anglers target snags deliberately. Once hooked, the fish will try to back into the snag immediately, and strong tackle is needed to counter this initial surge.

As well as taking dead fish off the bottom, eels will take live baits fished off the bottom after dark. Zander anglers on the Fen drains suffer problems with this, both with catching eels accidentally and, more often, by their baits being killed and partially devoured while still on the trace.

Grayling *(Thymallus thymallus)*

Recognition

The grayling cannot be mistaken for any other fish. It is a very beautiful fish with a huge, sail-like dorsal fin, and a silvery-blue streamlined body with delicate violet stripes. Grayling also have irregular dark spots on their flanks, as unique to each specimen as fingerprints are to a human being. As a member of the salmonidae family,

the grayling has an adipose back fin, which is a small fleshy protuberance situated between the dorsal and the top lobe of the deeply forked tail. The head is delicate, being small and pointed, and the mouth contains very tiny teeth with which it grips its food. They also have the scent of wild thyme, hence their Latin name, and make very good eating.

Habitat and Location

The large dorsal is intended to help the grayling to combat very fast flows, and this is the favoured environment of the species. They abound in clear, shallow, unpolluted chalk streams, happily co-existing with trout. Unfortunately, these beautiful fish are very sensitive to water pollution levels and as a result they are not widespread, living in pockets. The southern chalk stream tributaries of the Hampshire Avon and the Kennet, as well as the main rivers themselves, support a thriving population, as do some of the shallow, colder, faster-flowing streams of the north-east and north-west, and grayling are present in the border rivers of Scotland. Elsewhere, particularly in the Midlands, good grayling fishing is very hard to find.

Small to average grayling live in the shallow, fast glides in large shoals, with the bigger fish tending to hang on the creases between the fastest flow and more sedate water. The real specimens, as with other fish, are usually found in steadier, deeper water, where they do not need to expend so much energy and can live a lazier life.

LEFT: **A good grayling being brought to the net, caught on a wet fly in autumn. Grayling are often classed as coarse fish and caught trotting maggots and worms down a swim.**

Size

Grayling do not reach great sizes, and any fish over 1 lb (0.45 kg) in weight is a very worthwhile fish and a 2 lb (0.91 kg) sample a specimen. It is a rare angler indeed who has taken grayling over 3 lb (1.36 kg) in weight, and the current record of 4 lb 3oz, (1.89 kg) taken in 1989, will take an awful lot of beating.

Behaviour and Feeding Habits

The grayling's natural diet consists of small crustacea, nymphs, water snails, fish fry and any spent insects that drift by. They feed on the bottom but are quite happy to feed higher in the water during hatches of nymphs and mayflies. They group up in large shoals and, unlike roach, dace or chub, the coarse fisherman is unlikely to be able to entice them into a swim by regular feeding. Once they colonize an area they stick with it until they are ready to move on. The angler is well advised to spend time checking where they are feeding before contemplating fishing for them.

Grayling feed throughout the year but are at their best in very cold conditions, those clear, icy winter days when perhaps only dace are also willing to feed. In these conditions, they form very tight shoals and individuals tend at times to flash or splash at the surface. These are the signs to look for before starting to fish. Grayling are avid fly feeders, and all the methods appropriate for small river trout take their share of grayling. Leaded nymphs fished singly or a team of rolled nymphs are favourite methods of presentation but in the right conditions they will take the floating fly avidly and in the winter the Red Tag is the traditional pattern to try, fished either wet or dry.

If you want to fish a swim for grayling using coarse fishing methods shoals of grayling will respond to the stimulus of a regular supply of drifting maggots and casters; and trotting a float is the most enjoyable presentation. Initially, the grayling will often feed hard on the bottom but gradually feed at all depths as the competition for the loose feed warms up. This often will not apply to the biggest fish in the shoal, who will hang back and intercept any food item that trickles along the bottom past the rest of the shoal. These bigger fish are lovers of worms, and it is a good idea periodically to swap the maggot for a good-sized worm and run the float further downstream of the normal catching area.

Grayling of all sizes are always looking for aquatic nymphs shooting to the surface, and will often respond savagely to a trotted hookbait made to behave in the same way, by holding back the float so that the bait swings up in the water. Takes to this presentation can be dramatic.

TOP: A dry-fly fisherman plays a good grayling from a very thick bank.

ABOVE: Two good grayling caught trotting.

BELOW LEFT: The huge dorsal fin of the grayling shows clearly in the water.

BELOW: When autumn comes and the leaves start to change colour the grayling fisher comes into his own.

Perch *(Perca fluviatilis)*

Current Record
British **5 lb 9 oz (2.523 kg)**

Season
June to March in rivers, all year in stillwaters.

Distribution
Very widespread, perch are found in all waters.

Natural Diet
Fish, crustacea, worms and insect larvae.

Top Spots
For really big perch, reservoirs and gravel pits.

Top Tip
Perch are active feeders at dawn. It is best to start fishing at first light.

Recognition

The large mouth, boldly striped flanks, spiked dorsal and crimson anal and pelvic fins make the perch the most instantly recognizable fish in British waters, one that cannot be confused with any other. Although one species of perch is found in Britain, the worldwide perch family is extensive, both in fresh and salt water. Interestingly, they all share common features in the double dorsal fin, the first of which is spined, and the presence of spines on the gill covers.

The bold stripes and large eyes provide the best clues to the perch's predatory nature: the first gives the perch the necessary camouflage for stalking its prey and the second confirms that the fish feeds by sight. Whenever I look at a perch, I imagine an aquatic tiger. When threatened, or on the attack, the spiny dorsal is proudly erect, and it is thought that these spines are meant both to intimidate prey fish and protect the perch from larger predators, such as pike or catfish. It is not clear how effective this is, as I have found that in waters where both species are present, pike take perch readily without any apparent difficulty.

Habitat and Location

The perch is one of the most widely distributed species in Britain, thriving in muddy ponds, enormous lochs, stagnant canals, fast chalk streams, and every other type of water imaginable. An interesting fact is that the vast majority of newly flooded waters are first colonized naturally by perch, and this is thought to be caused by their extremely sticky eggs, which

(1.81 kg) fish a more realistic target.

The usual size of perch featuring in anglers' catches will be from tiny fish to 1 lb (0.45 kg), and many waters are prolific with fish in the 2–8 oz (50–225 g) range. These can be a nuisance to the angler setting out his stall for worthier quarry. The current record fish was taken in 1985.

Behaviour and Feeding Habits

The perch's aversion to strong light explains why it is an avid feeder in shallow water at dawn in summer, when light levels are low, and why it retreats to deeper quarters when the sun comes up. On gravel shallows on rivers and plateaux in gravel pits, perch are very active, attacking the hordes of fry that have spent the dark hours there. During very bright days, the bulk of a day's feeding will be done during the early hours.

In duller conditions, and during the cooler months, the feeding times are extended, with bottom-dwelling creatures such as crustacea and insect larvae, as well as worms, making up a progressively increasing part of their diet as fry become scarcer. Specimen perch have been taken with full-grown crayfish in their throats.

Perch are cannibalistic; in fact one of the best baits for a specimen fish is a baby perch. Use this knowledge to catch big perch in the summer, by fishing at first light when they are voracious. At this time, if a big perch is present, the small fish keep out of the way.

Perch use their natural camouflage in much the same way as a tiger hides in long grass. A big fish will spend much of its time motionless at the extreme edge of a rush bed, blending in perfectly with the reed stalks, waiting for small fish to swim past and the opportunity to pounce. Again, the angler can take good advantage of this behaviour, and the closer you can manoeuvre your bait to the rush bed, the more perch you will catch.

During cold spells in winter, big perch colonize the deeper areas, and this is when a legered lobworm fished in a deep hole in an estate lake, or presented on a paternoster under a deep undercut on a river bank, really pays dividends.

easily adhere to the feet or feathers of nomadic water birds, thereby transferring the species from water to water.

The large eyes of a perch, adapted for sight feeding in murky conditions, are, by definition, very sensitive to strong light, and this leads to their well-known preference for shaded places, such as overhanging trees, undercut banks, under thick weed rafts and so on. If you include deep water you have all the important clues as to where to look for perch. They are often found at significant depths in stillwaters, and bringing a hooked perch to the surface can often result in what is termed "gassing up". This is because, most unusually, the perch is equipped with a swim bladder minus an air duct, which means that it is able to acclimatize to pressure changes only very gradually. It is the same as a deep-sea diver surfacing too quickly and developing the bends.

Size

The current record is 5 lb 9 oz (2.523 kg) taken from a private lake in Kent, but any perch over 2 lb (0.91 kg) can be considered a very good fish, and a 3 lb (1.36 kg) fish, a specimen. A fish over 4 lb (1.81 kg) remains the unfulfilled dream of many a perch angler, although the recent dramatic upsurge in specimen perch across the country has made the capture of 4 lb

TOP: A gorgeous perch that clearly shows the huge, spiny, leading dorsal fin. This fish was taken from the Great Ouse on a brisk day in early autumn.

ABOVE: Three fine perch that were all caught on a legered lobworm in winter. In the winter months this bait really comes into its own as an attractor for perch.

OPPOSITE LEFT: An angler fishing close to the lily pads in summer. Lily pads are favourite haunts for perch, and the angler should fish as close to them as possible.

Pike *(Esox lucius)*

Current Records
British **46 lb 13 oz (21.234 kg)**
World **55 lb 1 oz (25 kg)** Germany

Season
Varies. Some waters all year, rivers June
to March, but in some waters October
to March only.

Distribution
Widespread in all waters.

Natural Diet
Fish, small mammals, worms.

Top Spots
Trout reservoirs such as Llandegffed,
Ardleigh and Ardingley.

Top Tip
Freeze deadbaits individually and
straight. They are then easy to use on a
cold morning and will provide you with
the maximum casting ability.

Recognition

The pike is the largest predatory fish found naturally in Britain. Its colouring is a perfect example of natural camouflage, as it harmonizes with the weeds where pike spend much of their time in ambush. It varies from deep olive on the back, through to a beautifully marbled combination of grey, green and yellow on the flanks, overlaid with a silvery sheen. The dorsal fin is set well back on the body, directly above the anal fin and, together with the large tail, forms a powerful propulsion unit giving the pike incredible acceleration from a standing start.

The head of the pike is unmistakable: long, flattened and

BELOW: **A fine pike caught spinning with a floating plug.**

BELOW RIGHT: **Spinning for pike off a sluice gate. This is a likely spot for these fish.**

equipped with the most fearsomely armed mouth. The upper jaw carries many rows of small, needle-sharp teeth, while the lower jaw has five or six large teeth on each side and rows of smaller ones between. The roof of the mouth and the tongue are also equipped with small teeth, enabling it to seize prey of up to 10–25 per cent of its own body weight.

Habitat and Location

Most rivers, lakes, ponds and pits in Britain contain pike, making the fish one of the most widely distributed. Specimens can as easily be taken from farm ponds as they can from huge Scottish lochs, and to many that is the appeal and mystery of pike fishing.

The pike is by nature a visual hunting predator, using whatever cover or camouflage it can to approach its prey undetected. It will be found lying among tree roots, in rush beds, and in the shadows of

trees. It particularly favours depressions in the bed where it can be inconspicuous, both in rivers and stillwaters. Favourite pike hot spots are the natural stream beds in reservoirs, as they are deeper than the surrounding water and the fresh water entering the reservoir creates a current that attracts fish.

In rivers, most fish seek out swims where fast water meets more sedate flows, known as creases. The river pike angler need look no further than a substantial crease swim. A steadier stretch immediately below fast rapids

can also pay dividends. Roach, dace and chub colonize such areas, and the pike follow them.

Size

There has not been the dramatic increase in pike sizes in recent times that there has been with tench and bream, and growth rates vary depending on the available food supply. Some of the deep trout reservoirs have seen unprecedented numbers of 30 lb (13.61 kg) fish taken, but the ultimate size fish, with the present record at 46 lb 13 oz (21.23 kg), is no bigger than might have been expected years ago.

The problem with pike is that artificial stocking with big fish rarely succeeds, as it does with carp or catfish, for pike invariably regress in condition when they are stocked. Second, pike do not enjoy pressure. When a large fish is caught, it is rarely allowed to live in peace. Other anglers pursue it, and eventually it will be caught once too often, or be badly hooked, and then it loses weight or dies. A 20 lb (9.07 kg) fish is still a super specimen and a 30 lb (13.61 kg) pike, the fish of a lifetime.

Behaviour and Feeding Habits

Pike rely on three senses to find their food: their sight when taking live fish, which they do at lightning speed; their sense of smell, for locating dead fish lying on the bottom; and their sensitivity to vibration, for detecting the fluttering distress signals of a wounded or dying fish. It used to be believed that the pike was never a scavenger, but now we know better. In fact, one of the most reliable methods of taking pike is the legered or freelined deadbait. A careful analysis of some records show that the fish caught using deadbaits are a much greater average size than those taken by any other method. All fish tend to get lazier as they get bigger, and a large pike uses a lot less energy taking a chunk of mackerel than it will chasing a sprightly roach.

TOP: **Pike anglers afloat at dawn on a reservoir. First light is a favourite time for both fish and angler alike.**

RIGHT: **Unhooking a pike. Pike have sharp teeth and proper disgorgers are an essential item of equipment for all pike anglers.**

Pike are instinctive attackers and can be goaded into action even when they are not hungry. If a noisy fish comes through a pike's field of view, creating a disturbance, the pike will often attack through sheer irritation. This is the basis of pike fishing with plugs, spoons and spinners.

Roach *(Rutilus rutilus)*

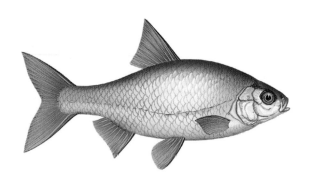

Current Record
British and World **4 lb 3 oz (1.899 kg)**

Season
June to March in rivers, all year in still-waters.

Distribution
Widely distributed in all waters.

Natural Diet
Aquatic insects, snails, worms, caddis, silkweed.

Top Spots
Chalk streams and large reservoirs.

Top Tip
Roach love the coloured water of flooded rivers. Try a big lobworm, upstream legered in a crease off the main flow.

Recognition

In colouring and shape, roach vary considerably between waters. At one extreme, the scales can be almost golden, although this is rare; at the other the roach is bright silver. Golden colouring is more likely to be found in big fish from gravel pits, whereas the bright silver roach is a typical inhabitant of the chalk streams. Generally, the body of a roach varies from blue-green on the back to dull silver flanks and a white belly. The lower fins vary from yellow to bright orange, the latter frequently leading to the common confusion between a true roach and a roach/rudd hybrid. The dorsal and tail fins tend to be reddish brown.

Physical recognition factors are important with big roach because they tend to hybridize with both rudd and bream. A true roach has 9–13 branched rays in the anal fin. This is the acid test between a roach and a roach/bream hybrid: the latter usually has at least 17 rays in the anal fin, and generally duller fins.

Roach/rudd are more difficult to distinguish, but the hybrids tend to have level lips, whereas roach have protruding top lips and rudd protruding bottom lips. The easiest recognition factor, however, is the relative positioning of dorsal and pelvic fins. In a roach, the leading edges of these will be level, whereas in a rudd or roach/rudd the dorsal is set back quite significantly.

Habitat and Location

Roach are very widely distributed throughout the British Isles, thriving in clear, fast rivers, gravel pits, canals, reservoirs and tiny, muddy farm ponds. They can grow to specimen size in all types of water, be it a barren pit or a weed-choked estate lake, so there is always the chance of catching a large fish.

Size

A roach over 2 lb (0.91 kg) is generally considered to be a specimen, and many waters do not hold roach as large as that. They become rarer as they reach 2 lb 8 oz (1.13 kg), and it is exceptional to catch a roach that weighs over 3 lb (1.36 kg). The current British record of 4 lb 3 oz (1.899 kg) was taken from the Dorset Stour in 1990.

Behaviour and Feeding Habits

The diet of roach is very varied, from water plants, aquatic insects and snails through to anglers' baits of all types. They will take bread in all its forms, meat and paste baits, maggots and casters, and large boilies intended for carp. Roach are particularly partial to worms, and a full-sized lobworm is a favourite bait for a big roach in

ABOVE: A 2 lb (0.91 kg) roach. This is the accepted size for a specimen fish, and many anglers may never catch a roach this size.

LEFT: The sun sets on a reservoir that is known to contain giant roach.

ABOVE: **A high, coloured river in autumn provides good conditions for large roach.**

RIGHT: **A good pole-caught catch of Irish roach. Occasionally the angler has a lucky day.**

coloured water. Roach are generally obliging feeders over a wide temperature range, from a hot summer's afternoon to a freezing cold winter's night. Small roach are not difficult to catch, ranging widely across all fisheries in large shoals, mainly in the shallower areas. As they get bigger they become more inclined to feed on the bottom, although this includes the shallows.

A noticeable trait in bigger roach, possibly due to increased caution, is that they become more nocturnal in their feeding habits, coming out to feed strongly at dusk as light levels decrease. Even in winter, they can be reliable night feeders. Big roach also love coloured water or floods, when conditions are similarly murky. The very biggest roach are often solitary individuals, or members of small groups, and these tend to favour deep

or steady water. In gravel pits, these big fish feed avidly over gravel bars, and over the gravel beds of feeder streams in reservoirs. Many reservoirs feature undertows at various points, caused by a combination of the flow of the feeder streams, wind action and pumping, either for domestic water supply, irrigation or canal top up.

These sub-surface currents are sought out by big roach.

In rivers, bigger roach also favour those shaded marginal swims beloved by chub, such as dense rush beds over gravel or raft swims under overhanging trees. They also seek out the gentler flows just off the main current and can be found close by in high water.

Rudd *(Scardinius erythropthalmus)*

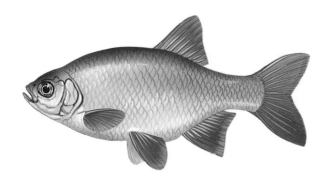

Current Record
British **4 lb 8 oz (2.041 kg)**

Season

June to March in all rivers, all year in stillwaters.

Distribution
Patchy, apart from Ireland. In England, neglected estate lakes, farm ponds and eastern-county gravel pits offer the best chances of finding good rudd.

Natural Diet
Avid surface feeder on insects, flies and moths. Also takes nymphs, midwater and insect larvae, and worms from the bottom.

Top Spots
Bedfordshire gravel pits and Irish loughs.

Top Tip
Rudd can feed at any depth in gravel pits. Fish with a slow-sinking leger coupled with a swingtip, so that a slow-sinking bait can be intercepted in midwater.

Recognition

Although similar in appearance to the roach, the rudd is much more richly coloured, as it is gold with crimson fins and has a bright yellow eye with a red spot. Although some gravel pit roach are more deeply coloured than their running-water counterparts, the fins are yellow-orange, quite different from the blood-red of the rudd.

Another distinguishing feature is the prominently protruding bottom lip, marking the fish as a surface feeder, whereas in roach it is the top lip that protrudes. The position of the dorsal fin is another clue as the leading edge is set behind the base of the pelvic fins, whereas in roach the

fins are level. Also, rudd display a distinctive pelvic keel, or sharp angle, from the pelvic fins to the tail. The lower body of a roach is altogether more rounded. The main difficulty in recognition comes about because of the rudd's tendency to hybridize, and this unfortunately is rapidly leading to a situation where true rudd are becoming rare. Some roach/rudd hybrids are almost indistinguishable from true rudd and it is extremely difficult for anyone to tell them apart.

Habitat and Location

As rudd are without doubt one of the most beautiful of all fish, it is a great shame that they are not more widely

distributed. Unfortunately good waters are rapidly growing fewer in number. There are a number of Cambridge-shire and Bedfordshire gravel pits that contain pure rudd, a handful of waters in the South East, and Ireland is still prolific. In all waters, however, particularly if they contain roach, the

TOP LEFT: A beautiful true rudd taken from a gravel pit.

TOP RIGHT: The River Shannon in Ireland. This is one of the most prolific waters where the angler is likely to catch a true rudd.

LEFT: A roach/rudd hybrid. It is very hard for anyone to tell whether a fish such as this is a hybrid or not.

days of the rudd sadly appear numbered. The only exception is secluded farm ponds, which often contain good rudd and no roach. If you find a water like this, keep it to yourself.

Size

It is doubtful that the present record of 4 lb 8 oz (2.041 kg), taken in 1933, in Thetford, Norfolk, will ever be bettered, not because rudd could not grow beyond that, but because it would be uncertain whether the fish was a hybrid or not. As roach/rudd hybrids grow bigger than either parent species, the record fish committee would have an impossible dilemma with a new claim.

Most rudd waters hold hordes of small fish, up to possibly 2 lb (0.91 kg) or more, while the better waters have a smattering of 3 lb (1.36 kg) rudd. This is the generally accepted measure for a specimen fish.

OPPOSITE: A reedy shallow bay in a secluded pond. Rudd love to feed on the surface, and this is typical rudd territory.

Behaviour and Feeding Habits

In traditional rudd waters, which include the large, shallow Irish loughs, secluded overgrown estate lakes and farm ponds, the rudd is predominantly a surface feeder, taking all manner of insects from the surface film. They move around in large shoals in big waters and are shy fish, often staying well away from the bank. On the Irish loughs, the method is to pole around the shallow bays very quietly until a shoal of rudd is seen "priming" – breaking the surface. Anchor at least 30 yards upwind and then drift surface baits to them under carp controllers or bubble floats. Big rudd become nervous quickly, and at most two or three fish can be taken before the rest of the shoal moves out of range. Then it is a case of upping the anchor and quietly following.

In the more intimate waters, rudd spend much of the daylight basking or feeding in the heavily weeded areas, venturing out as the light fades to feed around the fringes. The exception would be on an overcast, breezy day, when they follow the wind lanes,

picking off nymphs and midge larvae as they become available. Rudd, however, are not exclusively surface feeders, nor are they, as once was thought, only fish of summer.

The advent of gravel pits has shown that rudd are reliable bottom feeders and will take baits in the depths of winter, particularly in the deeper holes. Standard feeder tactics work well, one of the best baits being maggot-flake cocktail. In pits, it is very common to have several tiny fish and then one of 2 lb (0.91 kg) from the same shoal.

For this reason, it is a good idea to bait heavily when bottom feeding. One recommended technique is to use dead maggots or casters to preoccupy the small fish, and then fish over this with two or three grains of corn on a size 10 hook, or with a large piece of flake.

Of all specimen fish, predators apart, big rudd are the most prone to feeding midwater, and in deep lakes or pits it is common to find the rudd eight feet down if there is twenty feet of water. Depending on where you find them stationed, they can be fished for with float tackle set at the appropriate depth or by legering a buoyant bait, with the appropriate tail length. A deadly method is to use a buoyant hook bait in conjunction with a swimfeeder loaded with buoyant feed items. After the cast, hook bait and freebies rise at the same rate and you can often catch several rudd quickly using this tactic.

Tench *(Tinca tinca)*

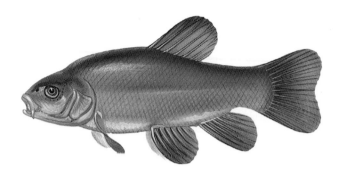

Recognition

The tench is one of the most instantly recognizable of our coarse fish. It may vary from olive green to deep bronze, with a lighter belly. Tench are covered in tiny scales with a very heavy mucous covering that gives them a pleasant satiny feel, quite unlike the mucous on a bream which comes away too easily. Tench fins are round and paddle shaped, the male being easily identifiable from the female by its cup-shaped ventral fins, at the roots of which are solid bands of muscle. Tench have two small barbules, one in each corner of the mouth, and bright red eyes.

Habitat and Location

Tench are very widely distributed throughout the British Isles, although they do not inhabit the fast chalk streams, except in the occasional sedate backwater. They are primarily fish of stillwaters or sluggish rivers, the traditional tench swim being a bed of lilies as dawn is breaking. They love to browse the margins, particularly where there are reed beds, and stay over the shallows in early summer, certainly until after spawning. Tench are one of the later fish to spawn, sometimes well into July, but do not seem to suffer loss of condition as much as other fish.

Gravel pits have provided an environment in which tench have done astonishingly well over the past thirty years.

Size

The size of tench has occupied the thoughts of many anglers since the 1960s, because of the incredible transformation that has taken place in that time, unique among coarse fish. For a long time, the record stood at 8 lb 8 oz (3.86 kg), a seemingly unattainable target as a 5 lb (2.27 kg) fish was very difficult to come by, and a 6 lb (2.72 kg) tench almost unheard of. But tench weights have increased dramatically so that today anglers regularly make catches that beat the old record. In any one season, hundreds of fish over 9 lb (4.08 kg) are recorded, and a fair number over 10 lb (4.54 kg). The current record is 14 lb 7 oz (6.549 kg) and astonishingly it is viewed as one of the records most at risk. It is now difficult to pin-point the size of an average tench, as waters vary so widely. Certainly, in the better waters, a tench under 7 lb (3.18 kg) now hardly warrants a mention, an incredible situation when compared to that of a generation ago.

LEFT: Portrait of a 9 lb (4.08 kg) tench showing the mouth of a bottom feeder and bright eyes. The size of tench has increased markedly since the 1960s, and fish such as this are now relatively common.

Behaviour and Feeding Habits

Although tench will take baits at mid-water and occasional ones are taken off the surface, they are primarily a bottom-feeding fish, moving round in large shoals and browsing areas like a flock of sheep. Their natural food consists of all types of insect larvae, molluscs, crustacea and worms, as well as some water plants, and they are particularly fond of browsing bloodworm beds. In soft-bottomed lakes, they love digging their snouts into soft mud and silt, rooting out their food, and at the same time sending up great clouds of bubbles. These are a classic indicator of tench activity. As tench gill rakers are very fine, bubbles from feeding tench are small and quite distinctive, resembling the froth on a washing up bowl. In these types of waters, where feeding is rich, tench are quite territorial, and their feeding times predictable. Generally early dawn is the best time, gradually tailing off by mid-morning

on a bright day. Large baits are taken confidently at first light; smaller offerings are taken much more circumspectly as the day wears on.

Gravel-pit tench are almost entirely nomadic, as their feeding sites are more widely scattered and probably need to be browsed in rotation. Their feeding times are also less predictable, and they can be caught in the middle of a blazing hot day, when tench of estate lakes are often totally unresponsive. Tench are seldom caught at night – early dawn is definitely the most reliable time.

ABOVE: Creating a new tench swim to be exploited at dawn the following day. It is a good idea to prepare the swim the day before and start fishing for tench at first light.

LEFT: Two massive early-season tench weighing over 9 lb (4.09 kg) each, both caught on maggots. Tench are reliable feeders over beds of particles, and lobworms and maggots are good baits for large tench.

Tench accept the usual range of baits and are particularly reliable feeders over beds of particles, such as casters or hemp. Maggots are a good tench bait and for stalking individual fish, nothing beats a big lobworm.

Tench are fish of the summer, and the first frost signals the end of serious tench fishing. They become semi-dormant and have little interest in feeding except on unusually warm winter days. Anglers that do target winter tench use only tiny baits such as single caster, which the tench take with great delicacy.

Zander *(Stizostedion lucioperca)*

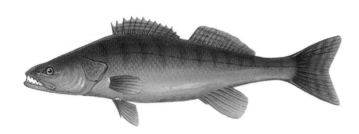

Current Records
British **19 lb 5 oz (8.76 kg)**
World **25 lb 2 oz (11.42 kg) Sweden**

Season
June to March in rivers, all year in stillwaters.

Distribution
Patchy, apart from the fen drain system. Other zander waters include the River Severn and Coombe Abbey Pool.

Natural Diet
Fish.

Top Spots
River Severn, the Fens, Coombe Abbey.

Top Tip
Fresh (not frozen) freshwater baits are best for zander. A good presentation is to fish a small, freshly killed bait popped-up off the bottom.

Recognition

The zander is a member of the pike-perch family, but it is a species in its own right, not a hybrid. It was introduced into this country from Eastern Europe. Streamlined like the pike, it shares many characteristics with the perch, such as the rough, slimeless scales and the double dorsal fin, the front one of which is spined. Like perch, zander are well adapted to feeding in low light conditions and have large eyes for this purpose. Some anglers have said that the huge, unblinking eyes are almost hypnotic! The large mouth is well endowed with small, backward pointing teeth, but the most obvious feature is the two long, front-mounted fangs, designed for stabbing and gripping its prey, which make the zander the vampire of the aquatic world.

Habitat and Location

Although there have been zander in selected fisheries since the 1870s, it was not until the release of 97 fish into the Relief Channel in 1963 that the species flourished and became of general interest to anglers. They rapidly spread through the associated drainage system and into the main River Ouse. The spread of zander still continues unabated, both through natural expansion and through illegal stockings. Some of the waters where the biggest zander are now found, such as the River Severn and Coombe Abbey Pool near Coventry, were originally stocked illegally. Despite this, the distribution of zander through the country is still very haphazard, with a bias towards the eastern counties, although that situation is changing rapidly.

Size

The present record, taken in 1998, is a colossal fish of 19 lb 5 oz (8.76 kg), and zander experts reckon that this could be beaten at any time by the first 20 lb (9.07 kg) fish. The Lower Severn is a short-odds location favourite for this. Generally speaking, most zander run from 2–8 lb (0.91–3.63 kg), and any fish over 10 lb (4.54 kg) is widely accepted as a specimen.

Behaviour and Feeding Habits

Zander feed mostly on small fish, up to perhaps 6 oz (175 g), although big zander have been taken on large baits intended for pike. They are pack hunters, attacking shoals of bait fish en masse and at speed, each shoal of zander comprising similarly sized fish. One of the features of fisheries containing zander is that the fish they prey on form denser and denser shoals for protection, leading to fears that they are being wiped out when in fact they have merely been more concentrated by the predators. As they get bigger, zander, like many other fish, become increasingly isolationist, and if you start catching small zander regularly it is not a good sign if a specimen is your quarry.

Zander share with perch a dislike of sea baits, although the odd big fish has accepted a smelt meant for pike; natural coarse fish, live or dead, are the baits to use. Small deadbaits fished hard on the bottom or livebaits fished

just off bottom are the favoured presentations, and one of the best deadbaits of all is a short eel section. Zander also share with perch a dislike of resistance, and frequently drop baits if the line is not free running.

The huge eyes give the clue to the preferred hunting conditions of zander, which are in low light. They are very nocturnal feeders in clear water, although high pressure and cold wintry conditions are very unfavourable as they are for many species. Zander are great lovers of brown floodwater, and will feed happily all day in these conditions. Autumn floods seem to be the best times, when they have recovered from spawning and the water temperature remains high after the summer.

The zander packs will obviously be concentrated where their prey fish are to be found, and this will often be around features such as bridges, and in the snaggy margins of stillwaters and around reed beds. The big Coombe fish are taken very close to overhanging foliage.

OPPOSITE: **Fishing for zander close to the margins. Zander hunt by sight and prefer freshwater bait.**

TOP LEFT: **A good zander is displayed.**

TOP RIGHT: **Unhooking a zander carefully.**

RIGHT: **A big zander, hooked at dusk, battles for its freedom.**

Baits and Groundbaits

During the summer months, some of the most effective fishing can be carried out with simple freelining, using natural baits. Natural bait fishing is mobile for the most part, moving from swim to swim, and is a recommended form of fishing for several species.

ABOVE: Cockles, prawns and shrimps all make good baits. They need to be fresh, not preserved, to be effective.

Natural Baits

From time immemorial the traditional bait for many species has been the worm. Worms and maggots are still favourite bait of many anglers and, certainly in the summer, more fish are probably caught on them than on anything else.

Lobworms and Redworms

The lobworm is one of the most universally effective baits, and one of the easiest to obtain. Choose a calm, mild night after steady rain and go on to close-cropped grass about two hours after dark. Use a torch as dim as possible and wear soft-soled shoes. You will see many worms lying completely out of their holes, and many more half in and half out. Grip the body adjacent to where it leaves its hole and pull gently without breaking it. Broken worms do not survive long in a wormery, and a dead worm will lead to the rest of the stock dying quickly. To keep lobs, you can use moist, but not soaking, garden soil. Every few days, place vegetable waste on the soil, and cover with damp sacking. If they are not overcrowded, and kept cool and damp, worms will keep in good condition for months.

The much smaller redworm is another excellent bait. You can ensure a good supply of redworms if you make a compost heap of grass cuttings, leaves, kitchen waste and animal manure in a shaded part of your garden. As the compost rots it becomes full of redworms.

Slugs

For summer chub fishing, the slug is recommended, the bigger and blacker the better. The only problem with slugs is that they can be very uncertain in supply and are difficult to keep fresh for long. It is best to collect them the evening before fishing, or, better still, at dawn on the day itself. On a dewy morning, you will find many slugs in the dampness of bankside vegetation, particularly round the roots of rushes and burdocks. Keep them as fresh as you can in a large bait box, out of the sun, with plenty of damp green stuff such as lettuce leaves to cover them.

ABOVE: Slugs collected early in the morning.

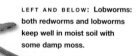

LEFT AND BELOW: Lobworms: both redworms and lobworms keep well in moist soil with some damp moss.

Cockles, Prawns and Shrimps

Prawns and shrimps are terrific baits, their problem being that they are extremely fragile, as well as being expensive. Always buy fresh, shelled cockles from a fish market. Do not buy them preserved or bottled, as they are kept in vinegar for human consumption. These are useless as angling baits.

Maggots and Casters

Maggots and casters (the maggot in its chrysalis stage) are among the most effective baits for all coarse fish, both in summer and winter, and much of their application will be in conjunction with the swimfeeder.

During the summer months maggots and casters are brilliant fished as a mass bait on rivers, when presented as a bunch on a large hook. The swim to select is one with a gentle flow, fairly close in, so the bait will not be unduly dispersed. It is also vitally important to loose feed with a bait dropper. The feed needs to be concentrated on the river bed at the selected fishing position, and the

Redworms

Maggots

ABOVE: All maggots can be dyed, and coloured maggots can be a most effective bait. Here curry powder has been used.

ABOVE: Small baits for summer fishing. Bread tipped with pinkies, sweetcorn, bread flake, a single maggot, casters, redworm and lobworm tail.

ABOVE: Two maggots mounted on a size 16 hook with gossamer monofilament line. Hook maggots through the tough skin at the blunt end and they will stay on the hook.

dropper guarantees this. For maggot fishing, so great is their pulling power, you can use them alone so long as you have sufficient quantity to achieve a level of preoccupation. You would generally need a minimum of half a gallon of maggots to fish this method most effectively. If you are concerned about them crawling away too quickly, they can be scalded or deep frozen before fishing. Dead maggots can be just as effective as live ones when used as loose feed although live maggots are recommended for hook baits.

For most angling applications, there are three important maggots. First there are the large grubs of the big bluebottle meat fly, the most common hookbait. Pinkies and squatts are the larvae of the greenfly and housefly respectively and, although these can be used as hookbaits, they are also widely used as particle attractors in groundbaits or for swimfeeder work.

If using casters, use them in conjunction with hemp, and fish them as you would any other particle bait. The only difference in approach would be that with some particles you should severely restrict the number of free offerings in the hemp, whereas with casters you should use a pint for every four pints of hemp. Obviously, mass baiting with casters alone would be effective, but the limitation to this approach is cost.

Pinkies

ABOVE: The well-prepared angler carries a range of bait and groundbait, including sweetcorn, bread flake, maggots, casters and lobworms.

Processed Baits

There are many processed baits available for the angler. One of the most common is bread which is used in several forms.

Bread

The tough crust on the outside of a farmhouse loaf is one of the best bread baits. Buy a fresh loaf from a bakery and if the crust is initially too brittle, seal it in a polythene bag. A few hours later the brittleness will have been replaced by crust so tough you will have trouble tearing it off the loaf. For hookbaits, tear off a piece of this crust, with a good chunk of flake attached, and fold it in half with the crust itself on the outside. Pass the hook through one side of the crust and out the other. When the bread is then released, it springs open on the hook. Thus mounted, you will find that the bait withstands any amount of twitching through the swim.

As well as mashed bread for loose feeding, you can also use handfuls of fresh, squeezed breadcrumbs to keep a swim primed; they disperse rapidly into attractive clouds as soon as they hit the water. For an even finer cloud, with minimal food value, liquidized bread is excellent. Remove the crusts from fresh, sliced bread and liquidize it in a blender. Liquidized bread is good for fishing in conjunction with a feeder, using bread flake hookbaits.

For fishing bread flake, use fresh, medium-sliced white bread. Tear off a strip approximately ½ in (1 cm) wide by 1½ in (4 cm) long and fold it round the hook shank, pinching it in place but leaving the point exposed. Fresh, sliced bread is also useful if you require a bread flake offering on a very small hook, where bread punches come into their own.

Bread is the most versatile bait. A loaf can provide a buoyant, sinking or neutral bait. Alteration of bait size enables the angler to change his presentation in an instant. With crust, increasing the bait size can provide a slow sinking offering, where previously the bait was nailed down to the river bed. With flake, a buoyant offering can be created by squeezing a disc flat on the hook shank. Where conditions are suitable for bread for winter chub, in all but very heavily coloured water, there is no situation where a bread bait can't be adapted to provide the ideal presentation.

Mounting Bread Crust on a Hook

1 Fold a piece of crust in half and pass the hook through both sides.

2 Allow the crust to spring open on the hook.

Mounting Bread Flake on a Hook

1 Fold a strip of flake from a sliced white loaf around the shank of your hook.

2 Squeeze the flake tight, squashing it on the hook, leaving only the point exposed.

ABOVE: Loading a feeder with liquidized bread. A feeder loaded with liquidized bread in this way is most effective when fished with bread flake hookbait.

ABOVE: Bread punches are useful to punch out small flakes of bread.

Sausage

Sausage was a much-used bait for barbel on the River Thames years ago, although many chub, roach and bream were tempted by it. There are two ways of using sausage: either a portion of sausage itself or a paste made of the meat. If using the sausage solely, it is best to use the skinned variety, as the skinless tend to be too soft and fall apart too easily. When using skinned sausages, however, take care to hook them in such a way that the skin does not impede hook penetration.

Sausage correctly mounted on the hook

Luncheon Meats

Luncheon meat is now one of the standard baits for many species, particularly chub and barbel. You can take good chub on all varieties of tinned meats, including luncheon meat, bacon grill, and chopped ham and pork. All these meats can be used successfully straight from the tin, and for chubbing use ¾ in (2 cm) cubes.

You must not, however, fall in to the trap of leaving the same bit of meat on the hook all day if there have been no bites. This is a common mistake made by anglers. Most meats of this type, if they have not been specially flavoured, soon lose their natural smells and become bland and very unappealing.

If you opt to use a flavoured variety of meat, the base brand does not really matter. The most important factor is the texture and toughness of the meat: it also must be tough enough to withstand casting without flying off the hook.

Many anglers use luncheon meat baits on ridiculously small hooks, and then complain that the meat keeps falling off. If you are going to use ½ in (1 cm) or ¾ in (2 cm) cubes of meat, use a hook matched to the size of the bait, a minimum being a size 6. To hook the meat, push the hook bend through the bait, and then twist and

RIGHT: Luncheon meat works well as a bait for many species, particularly chub and barbel, and can be both coloured and flavoured. Use a hook sufficiently large to keep the bait in place when being cast out.

ABOVE: Bread crust mounted on leger tackle. Carp and chub are often caught by fishing with bread baits.

RIGHT: A cube of luncheon meat correctly mounted on a hook.

pull the hook point back into the meat along a different line.

If you use this method of attaching the meat it will not fly off, and the hook will pull easily through on the strike provided you have selected your meat brand correctly.

Spicy Sausage

Sticks of spicy sausage meat, such as pepperami, are readily available from most supermarkets, and are convenient change baits, requiring no preparation and keeping indefinitely if they are in an unopened packet. Break off a chunk, flatten one end to put the hook through and you have a superb bait. As it has a tough skin, you need to pare this away with a sharp knife where the hook is to be inserted. If you wanted to experiment there are many other flavoured sausages that could be used as bait.

Mounted spicy sausage

Paste Baits

Paste baits are extremely useful and versatile, and have accounted for numerous fish. There are many ready-made pastes available and ones that can be made at home. The easiest to make are bread paste and cheese paste. It is worthwhile making your own paste and taking care to see that it is exactly the right consistency. As you become more practised, this is easier to achieve.

Bread Paste

Although waning in popularity, bread paste is an excellent bait and much cheaper than high-protein pastes. To prepare bread paste, you need sliced bread, without crusts, at least two days old. Fresh bread makes a lumpy, unappealing paste. Dampen the slices without oversoaking them, and squeeze out as much of the water as possible. Knead the paste in a clean, white cloth. If you knead by hand, the natural retained oil in your skin makes the paste an unappealing, grubby, off-white colour. The end result should be a smooth, white, pliant paste of even consistency.

If you want a variant from the standard bread paste, try adding powdered additives such as custard powder or strawberry blancmange powder. The list of potential flavours available is endless.

Meat Pastes

Meat pastes are superb baits for many species, the most common being made from sausage meat, finely chopped tinned meats or soft pet foods. You can make them up by mixing the soft meat with sausage rusk binder, which is available from butchers. However, you can mix the meat with any bulk binder that takes your fancy, and the delicatessen is full of interesting alternatives for you to try. Three of the most commonly used binders are breadcrumbs, biscuit meal and soya flour.

Cheese Paste

Probably the most common of all orthodox paste baits is cheese paste, which has accounted for numerous chub, barbel, bream, carp, tench and roach. Cheese paste can be made up

as follows. A 10 oz (284 g) pack of frozen shortcrust pastry is rolled flat, before being smeared with Mature Cheddar flavour. Then you add 6 oz (170 g) of grated mature cheddar and 4 oz (115 g) of finely crumbled Danish Blue cheese. The pastry is then folded over so that the cheese is inside and the whole rolled again. This is repeated constantly until thorough mixing has occurred, when the paste is formed into a large ball and thoroughly kneaded by hand. Put 2 ml of the Mature Cheddar flavouring in a large freezer food bag, put the ball of paste inside, seal the bag and then put it in the freezer until you wish to use it. When it is thawed, the paste has the most appealing texture and consistency, as well as a powerful cheesy aroma.

You can use standard bread paste as the base for your cheese paste, but using the frozen pastry mix is far more convenient and far quicker. It also gives the paste a lovely even texture that is a help when you use it.

During the summer months, when water temperatures are high, you can use cheese on its own, simply moulded into a ball on a large hook. In the winter, however, when the bait would be most used, all cheeses with

the consistency necessary for use on a hook harden considerably in cold water, and this impedes hook penetration. This problem can be overcome by making a paste as described on the opposite page, when the bait remains lovely and soft even in the coldest water.

Hemp Paste

Hemp paste is good for taking barbel and chub, and it is a particularly useful paste to have available as a stand-by. It comes into its own when fishing for these species in any river where there is a troublesome eel population. When plagued with eels, a switch to hemp paste usually solves the problem. For some reason, hemp is the one flavour that eels do not seem to relish.

You can make hemp paste in a similar way to cheese paste, using a base of shortcrust pastry. To make the paste, crush cooked hemp, making sure not to include too much of the liquid. You want the finished product to be a usable paste, and not something too sloppy. Mix the pastry with a little of the crushed hemp at intervals, until the consistency is right. It is easy to make the paste too wet, and then it is useless.

RIGHT: **A good leather carp that has fallen for some cheese paste. Most cyprinids take paste baits well.**

Making Cheese Paste

1 The ingredients: grated cheese, rolled pastry, cheese flavouring and colouring (optional).

2 Smear the pastry with the liquid cheese flavouring and then add the grated cheese and colouring.

3 Fold the pastry up and over the grated cheese. Roll it out again and then repeat the process.

4 LEFT: Knead the pastry and cheese together thoroughly until all the cheese has been completely absorbed and the paste has achieved an even, pliable consistency.

5 RIGHT: The finished paste, ready for the hook, with a portion rolled out as cheese balls. Put a 2 ml of cheese flavouring in a freezer bag and keep the paste in the freezer until you want to use it.

Synthetic Pastes

Commercial boilie mixtures can be used as very successful hookbaits in their soft paste form, although not all boilie mixes are smooth enough to form a paste suitable for a hookbait. Some of the fishmeal mixes are a little coarse in texture, and have to be boiled to work properly, when they are fine. There are many good quality ready-mixed pastes available in tackle shops. As well as fished on their own, they also make good neutral buoyancy cocktails when fished along with bread crust.

Making Synthetic Paste

To make up your own synthetic paste, a strong starting point is a high quality but forgiving base mix, such as 50/50 Promix. You then have to decide whether you want to add any more powdered ingredients, such as flavours, colours or sweeteners, or whether those ingredients will be in liquid form.

If you opt for powdered additives, such as curry powder or cheese powder, or natural extracts such as

powdered crab, mussel or nectar, these must be thoroughly mixed with the base mix before adding the mix to the binding liquid.

If based on a balanced 50/50 mixture, pastes can be made successfully with either water or eggs, but if you want the option of a hard-boiled bait as well as a paste, then eggs must be your choice. Even with a soft paste, eggs are recommended as they give the paste a lovely, pliable, waxy feel.

Beat the eggs thoroughly, add all the other liquids, flavours, oils or enhancers, and then add the powder slowly, mixing thoroughly as you go. Do not be in too much of a hurry. If you pile too much powder in and make the mix too dry initially, there is no way back. When you have a sticky ball of paste still too soft for hookbait, let it rest for five minutes. You will find that the paste tightens up in the air and becomes perfect.

If you plan to freeze the paste it also pays to make it a fraction soft. Pastes tighten up in the freezer. If you do not want the expense of buying

commercially available base mixes, paste baits can be made from a great number of products, such as trout and koi pellets, or tinned or dry pet food mixers, all of which are available from many stores and supermarkets.

Ingredients such as tinned pet foods, or tinned fish, are naturally sticky, and simply require a bulk binding agent to produce a workable bait. Kit-Kat chocolate bars mixed with fine breadcrumbs is a well-known example.

If you wish to base your bait on a dry ingredient, such as trout-fry crumb, any ingredients added to the bait must have a glutinous content to bind the powders in with the water or eggs. The simplest material to use is wheat gluten, but you should be careful not to use too much as this results in some very rubbery baits that can be unattractive to the fish.

Baits made with gluten can also be quite chewy, and it can be helpful to add a quantity of a light milk protein or baby milk powder. This balances the ingredients and makes the bait more palatable.

Particle Baits

The preoccupation of fish with large quantities of very small food items is well known, and occurs naturally, for instance when they feed on bloodworm colonies. To obtain the same effect with anglers' baits means saturating a small area with a sufficient quantity of particles so that the fish switch on to them exclusively.

Particle baits are those big enough to be used on their own or with two or three others on a big hook, and include sweetcorn, chick peas, maple peas, peanuts and tiger nuts. Mini-boilies are also considered particles from an angler's point of view.

Cooking Particle Baits

Particle baits must be used responsibly and you must always ensure that seeds, peas, nuts and beans are soaked or cooked well before use, so that they do not swell after they are consumed by fish, thereby causing distress. Cooking also prevents germination of naturally sprouting particles, but you only need to cook for a few minutes after pre-soaking. Overcooking will spoil the bait's attraction and negate the whole point of the exercise. Always keep the baits in the water in which they were prepared, as this maintains and progressively increases the flavour, but be careful to discard them if the baits start to smell sour.

Particles can be coloured and flavoured during the soaking and cooking process, by flavouring the water. As many synthetic flavours evaporate during boiling, it is best to stick to natural flavours and syrups, such as maple syrup, molasses, curry sauce or oxtail soup.

Using Sweetcorn

Sweetcorn is one of the most popular particles for many species, and there is little to be said about its preparation. Tins are better than frozen packets, as the sticky liquid enhances the attractiveness of the bait. Sweetcorn, if used in large quantities, is a bait that can become less effective for some species, such as tench, barbel and carp. When this occurs, changing the colour and/or flavour can give the bait a new lease of life. Corn takes flavours well, and a wide range of superb coloured and flavoured corn is available commercially from tackle shops.

Particle Preparation Guide

Tiger nuts, peanuts, cashew nuts, pistachio nuts, maize, red kidney beans

Soak for a minimum of 24 hours, and boil for 30 minutes or pressure cook for 20 minutes.

Tares, lupins, black-eyed beans, tic beans, maple peas, chick peas, soya beans

Soak for a minimum of 12 hours, and boil for 30 minutes or pressure cook for 20 minutes.

Hemp, dari, buckwheat, groats, rape, rice, wheat, barley, whole oats, millet

Soak for a minimum of 12 hours, then bring to the boil, remove from heat and leave in pan until cool.

Mixed particle feed, moth beans, mung beans

No soaking required. Bring to boil, remove from heat and leave in container for 24 hours.

Sunflower or safflower seeds, crushed hemp, maize flour, trout pellets

No preparation necessary.

ABOVE: This gives some idea of the range of baits required by a professional match angler. If the fish are not attracted by one form of groundbait, they may well be attracted by another, and it can pay to change mixes if your favourite is not successful straight away.

LEFT: Dried and prepared maize (sweetcorn). While it is cheaper to prepare your own in this way, sweetcorn is best used out of a tin, as the sticky liquid seems to add to its attraction. If you wish to flavour sweetcorn, then it is better to start with dried corn so that the flavours can be added as the corn is cooked.

Hempseed, dried and prepared

Crushed tiger nuts, dried and prepared

Uncrushed tiger nuts, dried and prepared

Chick peas, dried and prepared

Particle feed mass bait, dried and prepared

ABOVE: The most commonly used particle baits shown in their uncooked state on the left and prepared on the right. It is important to prepare all particle bait properly and care should be taken to follow the cooking times given in the information opposite.

Making Different Particle Rigs

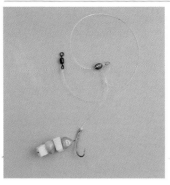

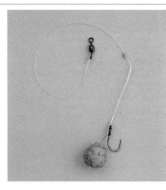

1 A pop-up rig with two kernels of sweetcorn with small pieces of sponge to float the rig off the bottom.

2 A slow-sinking rig mounted with one medium-sized tiger nut to explore various depths.

3 Particle rigs using sweetcorn as the basic ingredient: clockwise from the top; sweetcorn and redworm; dyed sweetcorn grain and maggots; four grains of sweetcorn on a hair rig; sweetcorn and luncheon meat; dyed sweetcorn and bread flake; centre, single grain of sweetcorn with casters.

Mass Baits

It is fairly obvious that you are more likely to create fish preoccupation the more small bait items you have. This points to mass baits, where individual offerings are far smaller than a standard particle such as a grain of corn. The most commonly used mass bait is hempseed, but others such as dari, tares, rice, wheat and pearl barley are also used.

There are two main hookbait choices when fishing over beds of mass bait: either a single large bait, such as a lobworm, or a cluster of the mass bait itself. One example is 20 hemp grains glued to a large hook, or strings of the bait glued to a hair or multiple hairs tied to the hook bend. Two of the better-known examples of using a large bait over a mass bait carpet are luncheon meat over hemp for chub and barbel, or a hookbait of large maggots over a bed of squatts.

One of the best mass baits available is mixed particle feed, from Hinders of Swindon, which is a mixture of many particle attractors. The information for the particle/mass bait preparation is shown opposite. Poorly prepared particles can be lethal to fish, so please take extreme care to follow the instructions given when you are preparing particles for fish.

Deadbaits

Deadbaits of sea fish are mostly used for pike fishing. The most common are herrings, sardines, smelts, sprats and mackerel. Among the best freshwater deadbaits are roach, small chub, an eel or lamprey section, small trout and immature pike. The best large sea baits are half a mackerel or a whole sardine. Sardines in particular are superb, but need to be frozen before casting, as they are very soft and otherwise break apart. In fact, most deadbaits are easier to use when partially frozen, for then they can be cast further. For this reason, a good cool box is an essential part of the pike angler's armoury.

When freezing deadbaits, always freeze them straight, wrapping each individually in a freezer bag or clingfilm. It also pays to cut them into sections before freezing if you intend using half baits. Cutting a frozen mackerel in half on a frosty morning on the river bank is no fun.

Among the freshwater baits, eel and lamprey sections are terrific baits. Eel tends to be best where there is a resident eel population, as the pike will gorge on them. Lamprey, however, is an enigma. Very few inland pike waters will have seen these creatures, and yet they really are superb baits. They are one of the few deadbaits that zander take regularly; they normally show a distinct preference for small livebaits.

When pike fishing with deadbaits, it is vitally important to carry a range of baits. There are plenty of days when, for instance, mackerel tail fails to produce a run, but smelts will take again and again. On one occasion a few years ago, it was impossible to get a run with half mackerel, but using a sardine would score success. After a few sessions, the runs on the sardine might stop, and it would become necessary to revert to big chunks of mackerel to start catching again. Size

A B O V E : The wise angler takes a good variety of deadbaits on a pike fishing expedition. Smelts, mackerel tail and sardines are all good baits.

preference is common, particularly when pike are feeding on fry in late autumn. At this time, large baits are often ignored, and you may need to use to small smelts or sprats.

Adding Flavours to Deadbaits

For several years many anglers have been treating deadbaits with various flavours and it can make a significant difference, particularly on big wind-swept stillwaters where sub-surface currents waft the scent trails far and wide. To flavour pike baits, pack each bait individually in a sealable sand-wich bag, having first poured a little of the chosen oil into the bag and thoroughly coated the inside walls. The bait is then frozen and the flavour impregnates the surface of the fish.

Before casting, always give the bait a further application with a paint brush so that, as well as being fully flavoured, it has an oily surface. This produces a characteristic oil slick on the surface as a pike crushes the bait with its teeth. On a calm day, this gives a very exciting early warning of a take. Try flavouring deadbaits with fish oils such as mackerel, smelt or eel. I have even taken pike on spice- and strawberry-flavoured deadbaits. It sounds all wrong, but it works!

Freshwater Deadbaits

The smaller, freshwater deadbaits, such as minnows, bleak, small roach or bullheads are attractive to zander, perch, eels, catfish, chub and barbel, as well as pike. Even bream and carp may cough up tiny roach when they are caught. In rivers, minnows are a favourite bait for chub, perch and barbel particularly in early season, just after they have finished spawning on the shallows.

Stillwater chub have a tendency to be very predatory and some of the biggest fish from the Oxford pits, one of the best places for chub, have been caught using a small whole mackerel.

More typically, though, large chub are fished for with medium-sized cubes or strips of mackerel flesh fished with a standard legering rig. Although this method is at its most efficient if you use a hair rig, as the firm flesh of the mackerel seriously impedes hook penetration.

TOP: Smaller deadbaits work best for pike when they are feeding on fry. They are also successful with a number of other species, such as perch, catfish and chub.

OPPOSITE: An angler's set-up to fish for pike using a deadbait.

Livebait fishing is usually practised for pike, perch, zander and catfish, although the use of live tiny fish, such as minnows, will catch chub and occasionally barbel.

The silvery fish, dace, chub and roach, weighing around 4–6 oz (115–175 g) make the best livebaits, although crucians make excellent pike baits and baby perch are a terrific offering for specimen perch. The biggest problem with livebaiting is catching the bait at the moment when you need it!

BELOW: A small roach makes an excellent livebait for many fish, including pike, perch, catfish and zander.

Boiled Baits

Boiled baits have become one of the standard offerings on many waters today, and there is no doubt they have revolutionized carp fishing. Although most anglers buy commercially produced "boilies", specialists tend to prefer their own mixes in order to maintain a degree of individuality and to ensure that the ingredients and preparation are exactly right.

If you decide to make your own boiled baits, there are two ways of going about it. Either you can add your own ingredients to a commercially available base mix, or you can take the trouble to prepare your own base mix as well. There are commercial base mixes based on bird seeds, mixed ground nuts, fish meals or milk products, or combinations of these. Some of these mixes will be balanced protein, often known as 50/50 mixes, and these contain high protein ingredients on a carbohydrate carrier such as semolina.

Some mixes will be high protein or high nutritional value bases. Other mixes will be intended for long life, others for instant attraction, and some will be more applicable to a particular season of the year. It is therefore important, before you buy your base mix, to discuss with your chosen supplier what you intend to achieve with your particular bait.

If you intend making your own base mix, there are extensive ingredients from which to choose. Find a combination that suits you and stick to it, or you will end up totally confused. Ingredients can include edible casein, sodium and calcium caseinate, lactalbumin, ground nuts of many types, mixed fish meals, soya flour, soya isolate, maize meal, ground bird seeds, rice flour, wheat flour, wheat gluten, oatmeal, ground pet foods and many others. In addition, there are various mineral and protein supplements you can add, such as codlivine, equivite and betaine. It is

possible to control the protein content of your finished base mix by selecting the appropriate ingredients from those available. However, in practice, some theoretical mixes cannot be rolled into usable baits, so experiment with small quantities first.

As a rule of thumb, milk products such as casein, caseinate and lactalbumin are high in protein, as are meat and fish meals. Low protein ingredients include most nut and cereal flours, although soya flour and wheat germ are of medium protein.

Making Boiled Baits

The first step is to mix the dry ingredients thoroughly, including any powdered colours, enhancers, sweeteners and vitamin supplements you have selected as well as the base mix. Second, crack your eggs into a large mixing bowl and beat them before adding any liquid ingredients, then beat the mixture again. The composition of your base mix will

Making and Moulding Boilies

1 The basic ingredients for all boilies are eggs, base mix and whatever flavouring you may choose.

2 Beat the eggs thoroughly and then add the flavouring; do not overdo this, a few drops is usually enough.

3 Mix in the base mix, adding a little at a time until you have achieved a soft, even-textured paste.

4 The finished paste. At this stage it will still be slightly sticky. Allow it to stand between 10 and 30 minutes to tighten up and become easier to handle.

5 Knead the paste well and roll out into sausages of the diameter that you require. Cut them into sections and then roll them into balls.

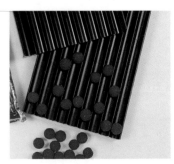

6 Alternatively, form the boilies into balls with a rolling table. These can be bought commercially and are useful if you are making a large number.

determine how many eggs are required, but you should use about four large eggs to 1 lb (0.45 kg) of dry mix. You may need as many as six eggs if you are putting together a high protein mix, which will generally be lighter and fluffier than a mix containing balanced proteins.

Add the dry mix slowly to the beaten eggs, thoroughly mixing with a wooden spoon, until a slightly tacky paste has been formed. At this point, rest the paste for about ten minutes and you will find that it tightens into a stiffer mixture that is pliable without sticking to your fingers.

Knead the paste well, and then break it down into conveniently sized lumps and roll it out into sausage shapes of the required diameter. Cut the sausage shape into sections of the required size with a sharp knife and then roll these into balls between the palms of your hands. As an alternative, if you intend fishing home-made boilies extensively, equip yourself with a bait gun and a rolling table, as this makes the laborious job of producing the boilies easier and faster.

Next "skin" the baits by dropping them into boiling water: generally between one and two minutes is sufficient. It is important that the water continues to boil, so do not make the mistake of trying to boil too many at once. For ⅝ in (16 mm) diameter baits, for example, 30 is the maximum number to cook at any one time, and the ideal receptacle is a large chip pan or something similar equipped with a wire basket. For those anglers who plan to make large quantities of home-made boilies the purchase of a specially designed boiler is a godsend, as you can skin large quantities at once. Having removed the baits from the water, allow them to cool and air-dry before attempting to put them into bags.

7 Plunge the balls into boiling water for one or two minutes. Do not let the water go off the boil.

ABOVE: An insulated bag, designed to keep frozen boilies (and other baits) cool during the summer, is an essential item in the angler's list of equipment. It is particularly important if you are on a fishing expedition and do not have the luxury of a deep freeze readily available.

LEFT: When the boilies have cooked, allow them to cool in the open until they have hardened, and then they are ready for use. If you do not plan to use them at once, you can freeze them. Place them in a freezer bag in small batches and then put them in the deep freeze. The illustration shows various boilies in different shapes and sizes ready for use.

A PVA bag rig with boilies and groundbait

Floating Baits

Many fish feed on the surface from time to time and can then be caught on a floating bait. It is always very exciting seeing a fish take a bait from the surface of the water, one of the pleasures of an angler's life.

Boilies

Boilies

Floating boilies, or pop-ups, are effective for any surface-feeding species. They are available commercially, or you can convert your own boilies to floaters by baking them in a hot oven or microwaving them for a short time. Alternatively, mould the paste round small cork balls before boiling them. When you mount the bait, use a very short hair rig so that the bait is touching the hook shank, or mount the bait in a special bait band sold specifically for surface carp fishing.

Baked boilies – pop-ups

High Protein Floater

A special sponge for surface fishing can be made by using a boilie mix with a double ration of eggs, to produce a runny mixture, and then baking this in the oven just like a normal cake. Different mixes give variations in floater texture: some are very light and open, while others give much denser results. Not all boilie mixes convert successfully to good floating mixes, and you have to go by trial and error.

Pet food mixers

Floating Pet Foods

Pet foods, particularly mixers, are extremely popular for surface fishing. They are a convenient size, visible at range, and retain their buoyancy for a long time. Pet food mixers can simply be glued to the back of the hook shank or fished in conjunction with a bait band. The mixers work best when the fish have been introduced to them for a while by prebaiting and have acquired a taste for them.

Carp pellets

Trout pellets

Koi Pellets and Trout Pellets

Fished in exactly the same way as mixers, koi and trout pellets are perhaps the ultimate floating bait for many species. Once fish begin feeding on them, they become totally preoccupied and a feeding frenzy can result, until the shoal is spooked by fish being hooked and landed. As they are smaller than pet food mixers, these pellets are best fished by gluing them to the hook shank.

Breakfast Cereals

Puffed wheat cereals will take surface-feeding fish such as carp, rudd and chub, if you use them in large enough quantities to attain preoccupied feeding. Being very light, they are best used on a calm day. Again, glue them to the hook shank but, as they are much less buoyant than trout pellets, it pays to add a small amount of rig foam to the hook. This prevents a waterlogged bait being dragged under by the weight of the hook.

Bread Crust

This is the most common and versatile floating bait of them all, ideal for both running and still water. In running water, when chub, dace, roach, rudd and possibly carp could be the target, it will be used freelined. For this application, a chunk of the tough crust from the outside of a farmhouse loaf is ideal. For mounting, fold a piece of the crust, flake inwards, pass the hook through the crust and then allow the bait to spring open on the hook. For freelining down a current, fishing with a greased line aids bait presentation by preventing sinking line causing drag.

In stillwaters, crust is often fished anchored in one spot for long periods, and for this application, particularly for big carp, a cube of stale crust, cut from the end of a tin loaf, will float like a cork and be highly visible.

Lobworms

Several years ago it was discovered that if air was injected into a lobworm it could be used on the surface as a bait for chub. This method has been extremely successful and taken many chub since, the bites being very savage. It is particularly deadly as the worm gradually becomes slow-sinking as the air slowly leaks out, giving the most natural presentation imaginable.

The slow-sinking lob could be the answer when fish are wary of normal surface baits. You should take immense care when injecting air into lobworms, and always keep the needle well away from your flesh. After use, always replace the needle guard immediately so that you cannot accidentally inject yourself.

Off-the-Shelf Baits

If you do not want to make your own boilies and floaters, then you can buy them at your tackle dealer.

Boilies

There are two types of commercially available boiled bait: frozen or shelf-life. As you might expect, the shelf-life varieties contain preservatives to keep them in good condition for long periods or until the packaging is removed. The quality of modern shelf-life boilies has never been higher, and there is no doubting their convenience, especially for the angler travelling abroad, where freezer facilities may be unobtainable.

Commercial boilies come in all sizes from mini baits of ¼ in (6 mm) diameter to giants of 1 in (25 mm), and they are also available as buoyant baits or pop-ups. There are many top-quality suppliers, whose boilies are all good quality.

Particles

Anyone wanting information on or a supply of particle baits need look no further than Hinders of Swindon. They keep all the popular particles, as well as supplying one of the best general mixed particle feeds available.

Most tackle shops sell packets of boiled hempseed and tares, and this is one area where tackle shops provide poor value for money. If you use these seeds in any kind of quantity, buy a sack from a seed supplier or a specialized outlet and prepare the seed yourself. As far as sweetcorn is concerned, you can use tinned corn from supermarkets but, if you wish to use it flavoured, Pescaviva corn, available from good tackle shops, is available in a superb range of flavours and colours, far better than anything you can produce yourself at home.

Groundbaits

There is a very extensive range of groundbaits available to the angler in tackle shops. If you are using pure breadcrumb as your groundbait base, however, try talking to your local bakery. You will often obtain a sackful of breadcrumbs or unsold loaves for a fraction of the normal cost.

Carp Groundbaits

There are now some excellent carp groundbaits available for use with method feeder tactics. There are high-

RIGHT: **Effective groundbaiting is essential when fishing for big bream.**

quality products available based on finely crushed hemp and other oily particles such as Nutrabaits carpet feed.

Pellets

Another tremendous growth area in groundbaiting is the use of pellets, particularly hemp pellets. Some manufacturers produce ball pellets to complement their boilie ranges: the idea is to create a similarly flavoured feed bed around the hookbait.

Base Mixes

There are many tremendous base mixes on the market, some of which are ready to use after adding water or eggs, and some which require the addition of other ingredients. Many of these are proven fish catchers. As well as base mixes, ready-made flavoured pastes in tubs are available from some suppliers. Although good, they sometimes offer poor value for money, as you can make the equivalent bait from a good base mix at a fraction of the cost.

Powders and Bait Soaks

As well as the vast range of flavours and additives now available, particularly successful additives are powdered attractants. Tikka powder and powdered extracts are excellent and catch a lot of fish.

Bait soaks or bait batters are commercially available, the idea being to make the hookbait particularly attractive among its fellows on the lake bed. For the mobile angler, convenient bait enhancement can be provided with spray flavours, and again there are many superb ranges.

Swimfeeders and Groundbait

ABOVE: **A bait rocket with particle bait and boilies.**

1 Various swimfeeders are designed to allow the chosen groundbait to trickle out at the correct rate.

2 Here a swimfeeder has been filled with fine particle groundbait to be used for bream.

Flavours, Colours, Enhancers and Oils

Although many baits can be modified with common foodstuffs found in all kitchens, such as dipping bread flake in honey, or smearing crust with cheese spread, this section is devoted to those synthetic products used for bait enhancement that are available from tackle shops and bait suppliers.

Flavours

Most commercial flavours come in highly concentrated form, and it is an easy mistake to overdose your baits. This will repel fish rather than attract, as it renders the bait bitter. Very rarely is it recommended to use more than ½ fl oz (5 ml) of flavouring per 1 lb (450 g) weight of synthetic bait. If you wish to add flavours to orthodox baits such as bread, maggots or luncheon meat, it is better to be sparing, rather than too liberal.

Most manufacturers give instructions on their containers, or in brochures, on dosage levels that you should follow. Exceeding these levels may give a very short-term attraction for fish, but the bait will soon blow.

For flavouring bread, for crust or flake fishing, put about ½ fl oz (5 ml) of the flavour into a large freezer bag, coat the sides with the liquid, put the loaf inside, then seal and freeze. When the loaf thaws, it sucks in the

flavour. You can flavour breadcrumbs and liquidized bread the same way, while mashed bread is treated simply by adding the flavour to the water during the preparation. To flavour maggots, put ½ fl oz (5 ml) of your chosen flavouring in the bottom of a bait box, with a small amount of water to spread the flavour, introduce the maggots and then give the box a vigorous shaking. After a few hours, the box should be dry, as the maggots will have absorbed all the liquid.

It is better to flavour maggots with powdered products, such as turmeric or curry powder, as you get a more even flavour distribution. Sprinkle the powder liberally over the bait and let the maggots continually work through it. Powdered flavours are also useful for coating naturally moist baits such as luncheon meats.

If you wish to use liquid flavours with meats, you can either simply soak or gently fry the meat with the chosen flavour in an old frying pan. Do not fry for too long, however, as one of the attractions of meat is its natural fat content, which will then be lost. A good ploy with luncheon meats is to dampen them with a flavour enhancer, and then coat with a chosen powder. Freezing locks the flavours into the bait and ensures that the bait on your hook will retain its attraction for several hours.

Colours

It is rare that a coloured bait gives any significant advantage over a natural one, and some anglers tend to use colour as a means of identifying different bait batches. Having said that, dark baits can be useful on very bright days in clear water. For instance, barbel have been known to shun pink luncheon meat and then take confidently a piece dyed black, or to take dark red corn after appearing terrified of normal yellow corn.

Some carp anglers swear by brightly coloured baits on dark lake beds, and some pike anglers have great faith in coloured deadbaits. Whatever the truth of the matter, colour will only be significant in water under about six feet deep. At greater depth than that, most colours appear the same.

Enhancers

There is a whole range of flavour enhancers, vitamin supplements, sweeteners, appetite stimulators and bulk food oils, and it is very easy to become confused. They are mainly used with synthetic carp baits, and the best thing to do is to select a small number and try to stick to them.

As with all these types of product, the manufacturer's advice is crucial. As a general guide, add sweeteners

TOP: Dyes for colouring baits. This is really only significant when fishing in shallow water.

LEFT: The range of flavours and additives found in tackle shops can be confusing to the beginner. Choose just a few to start with.

and appetite stimulators to naturally sweeter flavours such as strawberry and molasses, while the sweetener can be substituted with a savoury flavour enhancer when using flavours such as cheese, spice, fish or meat. Many baits, sweet or savoury, are also enhanced by the addition of a little salt in the initial dry mix.

Essential Oils

These oils are highly concentrated natural plant extracts to be used with care and very sparingly. Examples include geranium, peppermint and Mexican onion. These products are used in concentrations no greater than a few drops per pound of base mix as they are so powerful.

Many carp anglers who prepare their own baits for long-term use, without that bait blowing, use essential oils on the best quality base mixes, and then keep the recipes strictly to themselves.

TOP: Deadbaits can be both coloured and flavoured and this adds to their attraction.

ABOVE: Colour is a useful way of identifying batches of the same bait. Here cockles have been dyed red, yellow and orange.

Groundbaits and Prebaiting

Groundbaiting means introducing free offerings or a food carpet in a selected area just prior to, or during, the fishing session, while prebaiting has come to mean the preparatory work carried out hours, days or even weeks before the swim is fished. There are many reasons why prebaiting is important. First, it can be used to concentrate fish in the area in which you wish to angle. Second, by allowing the fish time to feed on your bait unmolested, it can make catching the fish easier when you do introduce a baited hook. Lastly, it can wean educated fish on to a bait of your choice, giving you an important edge over other anglers.

Groundbaits

There are endless varieties of groundbaits, varying from fine powdered cereals to mixed particles, or combinations of both. If you wish to stimulate a feeding response to hookbaits, without necessarily feeding the fish, then a pure powdered cloud groundbait is ideal. This would be the common choice for a match angler seeking large numbers of smaller fish. A cloud bait can range from a simple mix of very fine pure breadcrumbs to a complex mixture of meals and attractors designed for specific purposes and different species. Tackle shops are full of products to meet every angling requirement, and you can buy heavy mixes for rivers, light fluffy mixes for canals, bream mixes, carp mixes, and so on.

Specialist anglers seeking bigger fish would more commonly use a combination of meals and particles, particles only or, for carp anglers in the main, beds of boilies. An example of the first category is the tench or bream angler who uses brown breadcrumbs as the bulk carrier, mixed with particle feed such as hemp, corn, rice, pearl barley, casters or maggots. The second category includes the barbel angler preparing a swim with hemp and corn, or the carp angler laying down a bed of tiger nuts.

Mixing powdered groundbaits is critically important, since you want the bait to be neither too sloppy nor too stiff. For bottom-feeding fish in an estate lake, for instance, you want the bait to hit bottom without breaking up, but then quickly disperse into an appealing carpet. For good control of the mixing process place the dry bait in a wide bowl, remove any lumps, and then add the water plus any liquid additives very slowly, mixing as you go, until the required consistency is obtained.

Match anglers use a sponge to sprinkle water evenly over the dry ingredients, and this does give very

Preparing Groundbait

1 The dry ingredients for groundbait. These may include breadcrumbs, particle feed, hemp, sweetcorn and various meals and attractors.

2 Mix dry ingredients together in a bait bowl. Turn the mixture over a number of times to make sure that all the ingredients are evenly distributed.

3 Add water to the mixture. Do this slowly and continue to turn the mixture over as the water is added. It is important to keep an even texture.

7 To bait a swim, take a handful of groundbait and form it into a ball. You may have to add more water to your mixture as the day wears on.

8 The ideal ball is about the size of an orange. Throw it into the water by hand if you are baiting close by. For longer ranges use a bait catapult.

close control. A perfect ball of groundbait should hold together easily without being sticky, but then crumble down into the consistency of damp pastry crumbs. The same bait for river fish could be made slightly stiffer so that, instead of actually breaking up on the river bed, it gives off a constant cloud of attraction which is then washed downstream.

Prebaiting Techniques

Balls of groundbait are generally introduced either by hand or by catapult, and this is where it is important to ensure that the bait does not break up in flight. The more accurate your bait placement, the more efficient your angling. If you have access to a boat or bait boat, your bait can be sloppier, mashed bread for instance, as it will sink straight down to the bottom. For prebaiting particles, if you are baiting

at close range, say with hemp for barbel, the bait dropper is an invaluable aid and allows very accurate placement of the bait. For prebaiting particles at range, the bait rocket or spod is a useful tool. This is a cylinder with buoyancy at the base. It is filled with particles, cast on a strong rod and heavy line, and turns turtle as soon as it hits the water, depositing its load of bait in the required spot.

A similar principle is used with the baiting cone, which is designed to introduce a combination of particles and loose groundbait to the fish. Again, the cone is filled with the particles, the wide top sealed with a groundbait plug, and the lot cast to the desired spot.

For prebaiting with boilies at range, the two most commonly used methods are with the catapult and the throwing stick, although more and

more carp anglers are investing in radio-controlled bait boats for faster baiting at long range. Catapults require little explanation, but the throwing stick is an accurate tool for boilie placement after a little practice. To be proficient, it is vital that your boilies are perfectly round and the same size, or you get baits flying in all directions and to all ranges. This defeats the object of prebaiting, which is to concentrate fish in a fairly tight area. A special rolling table is a help towards achieving standardization if you are making your boilies at home.

Even pike anglers can employ prebaiting techniques successfully, constantly feeding likely areas with small pieces of fish. It is rarely necessary to bait at range, as big pike are reliable margin feeders, particularly around overgrown banks or in marginal reeds where they lie in wait for their quarry.

4 Keep working the groundbait until you are satisfied that everything is thoroughly mixed and you have achieved the right consistency.

5 The finished mixture should resemble damp crumbs. With experience you will be able to achieve this texture without difficulty.

6 Perfect groundbait should hold together under light pressure but break down easily into light crumbs without lumps when in the water.

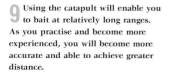

9 Using the catapult will enable you to bait at relatively long ranges. As you practise and become more experienced, you will become more accurate and able to achieve greater distance.

Equipment

Before choosing expensive equipment or tackle, such as a fishing rod, be sure that it will perform the task you ask of it and give you pleasure in its use. There are many factors to take into account, such as the species you hope to catch, and the size, the casting weight and distance involved, line strength and so on. Having determined the suitability of the rod, you then need to ask yourself whether its action is to your liking. For example, you may never have been a fan of fast-tapered rods, but if you need to pick up line at long distance in order to set the hook, you have to compromise, and a fast-tapered rod is the best for this.

There are three types of action. The first, "through action", is where there is a uniformly smooth curve through the blank when playing a fish, and there is no doubt that maximum angling pleasure is to be had with a rod of this type. Where a little more backbone is required, "progressive action" rods come to the fore: with these a modest fish will still give a pleasing bend in the rod but there is a progressive power build-up in the butt to control larger specimens. Lastly, there are "fast taper" rods, that are very stiff in the butt and have very flexible tips. These are designed for ultra-long casting and fast line pick-up.

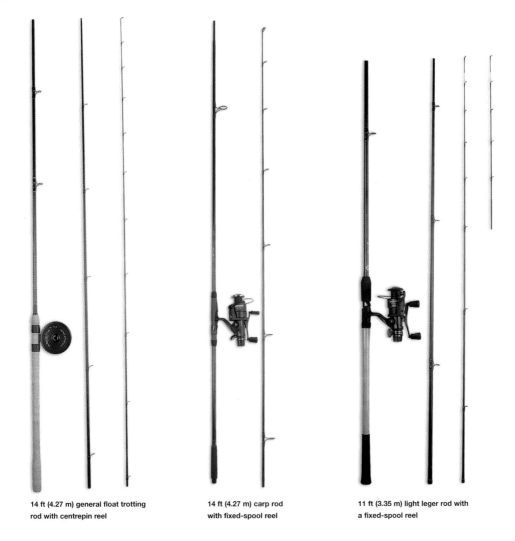

14 ft (4.27 m) general float trotting
rod with centrepin reel

14 ft (4.27 m) carp rod
with fixed-spool reel

11 ft (3.35 m) light leger rod with
a fixed-spool reel

Type of Fishing	Recommended Rod
	(all progressive action except where stated)
General float trotting	14 ft (4.27 m) Drennan IM9 float rod, 12 oz (0.34 kg) test curve
Float fishing for bigger fish	13 ft (3.96 m) Harrison Supreme Specimen float rod, 1 lb (0.45 kg) test curve
General barbel fishing	TM 11 ft 3 in (3.45 m) Century Pulse Barbel rod, 1 lb 6 oz (0.62 kg) test curve
Upstream barbel fishing	TW 12 ft (3.66 m) Century Pulse Upstreamer rod, 1 lb 12 oz (0.79 kg) test curve
Short/medium-range carp/pike	12 ft (3.66 m) Harrison Supreme carp rods, 2 lb 4 oz (1.02 kg) test curve
Long-range carp	12 ft (3.66 m) Harrison Supremecarp rods, 2 lb 8 oz (1.13 kg) test curve
Pike deadbaiting	13 ft (3.96 m) Century Armalite rod, 3 lb (1.36 kg) test curve
Big chub	11 ft (3.35 m) Century Pulse chub rod, 1 lb 4 oz (0.57 kg) test curve
Light leger, roach, medium chub	11 ft (3.35 m) Shimano Aero Quiver rod, 1 lb (0.45 kg) test curve, through action
Medium/long-range feeder	12 ft (3.66 m) Harrison Supreme feeder rods, 1 lb 8 oz (0.68 kg) test curve

An all-round coarse angler will need several rods in his armoury to deal with different angling circumstances. The list in the list above is recommended, but there are many other excellent manufacturers and rods for the angler to choose from. Buy one rod at a time and expand your range gradually.

The "test curve" is the weight required to pull the tip of the rod to an angle of 90 degrees to the butt. It gives an indication of the weight the rod is capable of casting.

Reels

There are three basic types of reel that any coarse angler needs in his or her fishing bag.

Fixed-spool Reels
These are the most common in popular use. For barbel and tench fishing, feeder work and stillwater float fishing, the Shimano Aero GTM 4010 is a good choice. It has three spools of varying line capacity. The reel features a double handle dyna balance system. This is delightful in use, giving a smooth, vibration-free retrieve. Tapered spools and a two-speed crosswind line lay system ensure that casting is smooth. The GTM 4010 is fitted with a fighting drag system, a two-stage clutch mechanism allowing clutch tension to be varied during a fight.

A delightful little reel to use in conjunction with the Shimano Aero Quivertip rod is the Aero 2000.This is very light, well balanced and has the most delightful clutch.

For carp and pike fishing, where fast runs often take yards of line, the larger GTM 6010, holding a much greater capacity of heavier lines, and which features the baitrunner system, is recommended. This allows fast-running fish to take line in free spool manner with the bail arm closed – important in preventing tangles.

Centrepins and Closed-face Reels
Centrepins are usually preferred for trotting, but a closed-face fixed-spool is good if conditions are difficult due to strong winds.

Many anglers use centrepin reels for legering for barbel, using an audible check for bite detection. If you have difficulty casting, Ray Walton markets a centrepin that swivels so it casts like a fixed spool but then reverts to fishing as a traditional centrepin. If you only use the centrepin for legering, this is a good choice.

Multipliers
Where you need a large capacity of heavy line, say for trolling for pike or fishing for big catfish, a multiplier reel is usually best. However, before buying one, ask your tackle dealer for advice.

201 multiplying reel

Centrepin reel

GTM 6010 reel with spare spool

4010 reel

Clothing

The best angling outer garments will be light, comfortable, breathable and yet 100 per cent waterproof.

There is a large range of suits, jackets and trousers, and a bib and brace coupled with the three-quarter jacket gives complete versatility, whatever the weather conditions. A jacket with a detachable hood is recommended. Jackets with a bib and brace are also very convenient. Three-quarter jackets with a separate zip-out quilted lining that can be worn independently, are also available.

Always purchase outer garments at least one size too big, to allow for a one-piece thermal suit or thermal underwear underneath in the depths of winter.

In winter, the body loses heat fastest through the head, hands and feet. Always wear a good hat: a wide-brimmed waterproof trilby, with chin straps, for rain and wind, and a woolly hat or a balaclava for very cold days are well worth the money.

Waterproof jacket and trousers

Fleece hat and gloves with waterproof trilby

Gloves and Waders

Neoprene gloves are some of the warmest angler's gloves available. For mobile fishing, the fingerless gloves are good, while the cut finger variant is appropriate for more static fishing, say for pike. With these, the whole hand is covered, but for rebaiting the first two fingers and thumb of the glove can be folded back and kept in place by Velcro.

The variety of weather, water and temperature conditions demands a wide selection of footwear for maximum efficiency and comfort. For summer, Derriboots, thigh or chest

Fishing jacket

waders, and for winter thermally lined moonboots or thigh waders are recommended. Neoprene chest waders are also excellent. Several spare pairs of socks, some thermal, should always be to hand, as should a couple of towels. Wet and cold feet in winter is a recipe for misery.

Nets

Landing nets and keepnets should be constructed of the softest material available, thus preventing any damage to fish. For pike, carp, barbel and catfish the Relum Be Safe triangular landing net, with 3 ft (1 m) arms is recommended. For heavy fish, you can use the Relum Springlok system, which allows the mesh frame to be detached or folded back when a fish is landed, thereby taking strain off the handle and making fish carrying easier. The mesh also features weighing straps, to avoid undue handling of the fish which can be weighed in the net and then released.

There is an option of a mixed mesh, so that a very fine mesh cradle makes up the net base. This is a godsend where hooks are prone to become tangled, for example trebles used in piking. This version is good for stillwaters, but in river work, say for barbel, a plain mesh net is better as the fine variety offers great water resistance in a fair current.

Another option is a net with a telescopic handle, which is useful as you are often faced with high banks or wide rush margins.

For smaller species, particularly on rivers, spoon-shaped landing nets are preferable as they are less prone to tangling in vegetation. Where spoon landing nets and keepnets are concerned, some of the best products are marketed by Keenets. The big mesh Mega Spoon for mid-size species, such as chub and tench, and a smaller, pan net version with a duplex mesh for roach and rudd are both recommended. Again, it is worth using a telescopic handle, such as a

Wellington boots

Some of the various types of keepnet that are available.
FAR LEFT: Waterline square keepnet; LEFT: Round keepnet.
ABOVE: Smaller keepnets are suitable for short-term fish retention.

ABOVE: An unhooking mat.

carbon telescopic which extends to 10 ft (3 m). Coupled with a lightweight spoon frame, the whole net is simple to use single-handed. But do not attempt to lift a fish at the end of 10 ft (3 m) of carbon, or you could break the handle. Ship the handle towards you and lift out the fish by grasping the net frame itself.

With regard to keepnets, buy the largest and softest net your budget allows. But use it responsibly, keeping it pegged out in a good depth of water, in uncrowded conditions, and for the minimum time possible.

Weigh Slings, Retention Systems and Unhooking Mats

Most specialist anglers retain a fish they wish to photograph in a carp sack, and there are many excellent products available. The most useful are the sack/weigh sling combinations. They are lightweight, compact and soft enough to stuff into small spaces in seat boxes or rucksacks. Also, always have handy a couple of old guy ropes and bivvy pegs, to ensure a fish can be retained in sufficiently deep water.

Under no circumstances place more than one fish in a keep sack, and when pegging it out in water always ensure that the material is not trapping the fish's gills. In hot weather, particularly where there is only shallow water in the margins, ask yourself whether you should use a sack in the first place. The welfare of the fish should be paramount.

For retaining big fish in running water, make sure that the fish lies with its head upstream and that the sack is not twisting in too strong a flow. A steady throughput of water should be the intention.

Far better, though, in rivers, is a system that can be pegged out into a rigid structure that allows a fish to breathe normally and recover properly. The Queenford retention system, a rectangular structure made of very soft sacking material with mesh ends for ease of water flow is recommended. This also has a zip top so that once the sack is in place, it does not need to be disturbed. There are similar pike tubes available commercially.

This idea has now been extended to smaller versions for barbel and large specimens of catfish. Again, the zip top allows ease of access.

It is very important that some fish be retained for a short while to allow them to recover in safety. This is particularly true of barbel that fight themselves to a standstill, and also big bream for which the Queenford system was originally designed.

Unhooking mats are important to use when banks are hard and irregular. This is particularly true of gravel pits. There are many good products about.

ABOVE: A combined sack and weigh sling is essential if you want to weigh your catch without doing any damage to the fish.

Umbrellas and Bivvies

The all-round coarse angler will often require shelter from the elements, and there is much superlative equipment available. Shelters range from the standard umbrella through to the portable detached bungalow. For river fishing, if you are adopting a mobile style, it is better if possible to forego an umbrella, as it discourages moving swims. It is far better to rely on good-quality protective clothing and waterproof luggage.

However, if you intend to spend reasonable time in one swim, an umbrella can provide much greater comfort. For tight swims or on sloping banks, the standard umbrella is fine. If you have a little more room there is a lightweight pop-up bivvy available on the market that erects in about 15 seconds and has sufficient headroom for a seatbox. It has two securing bivvy pegs and special retaining sleeves on the side panels for bivvy poles to give it extra rigidity in rough weather, and two zip-out rear panels to accommodate pole anglers.

For the longer-stay angler on stillwaters, there are many good bivvies. The umbrella/bivvy hybrid, which can be used as an umbrella, is superb when the Velcro-equipped storm sides are added. It is excellent for a short overnight session.

Where a longer stay is planned, and comfort is more of a requirement, one of the new double-skinned super bivvies with built-in groundsheet is

ABOVE: A good modern bivvy protects the angler from the elements.

A standard angler's umbrella

the answer. These are available with extended groundsheets into the porch area, side ventilators, mosquito nets, rain skirts, and inner and outer doors. Some even have rear doors, clear section windows on the doors, side panels or storm sides. Some bivvies have extended front tunnels to store cooking and lighting equipment, boots and wet clothes.

Folding Chairs and Bedchairs

For long sessions, a low chair is recommended. The most comfortable chairs should be fully sprung and feature high-density foam inserts for total cushioning. As well as seat padding, a good chair might feature generously padded head, leg and arm supports, so preventing the metal frame causing any discomfort. Chair legs should fold flat and be light, making the chairs simple to transport. Each leg should be independently adjustable to cope with uneven banks, and fitted with a non-slip rubber foot.

With all low chairs it is necessary to prevent the feet sinking into very soft mud. The best models feature anti-sink wide feet, which work well most of the time. For those occasions, however, when the banks are very soft, you might want to carry four old carpet tiles to place under the feet, as they keep chairs stable even in boggy conditions.

A lightweight folding chair for the roving angler

For overnight sessions, a bedchair will be required. Better ones fold completely flat, have three sets of adjustable legs for extra stability and a very firm locking mechanism to put the head rest in any position required. This is important as it allows the product to be used as a chair when fishing and then it converts to a bed for sleeping.

Seat Boxes

For mobile fishing you may prefer a seat box to a chair. This cuts down on the amount of gear to be carried. When fishing a swim where continual float casting is required, a seat box is often more convenient than a low chair simply because it is higher. In these circumstances, extra comfort and convenience are provided by seat boxes with trays housing all the paraphernalia you are likely to need.

ABOVE: A bedchair is essential for the long-stay angler.

Hooks

There is a wide choice of hooks and patterns available from many manufacturers. There is simply not enough room to compare each manufacturer's hooks in depth, and for simplicity the hooks discussed all come from Drennan which supplies all the patterns that any angler is likely to require.

There is much debate about the merits of barbed versus barbless, mechanically or chemically sharpened, round bend versus crystal bend, straight point or beak point, and so on. The best advice is to experiment with patterns until you find one that suits the particular style of fishing in which you are engaged. For instance, where you wish to stop a big fish from reaching a snag, a forged beak hook will resist pulling out, whereas you may lose fish after fish on chemically sharpened or barbless patterns. On the other hand, a chemically sharpened pattern such as Super Specialist could be the choice if you want good long-range hooking, where you have room to play the fish without undue pressure.

If you wish to use barbless hooks at all times, Specimen Barbless and Carbon Barbless are excellent. The table at the foot of the page shows the hooks recommended for various fishing styles.

Disgorgers

Super carbon maggot hooks tied to nylon

Hook tyers

Coarse fishing hooks

Size 10   Size 12   Size 14   Size 16   Size 18   Size 20

Style of Fishing	Hook Choices	Comments
Big Carp	Sizes 2 to 6, beak point, in-curved	Continental boilie
Pike	Sizes 4 to 8, barbed treble hooks	Extra strong
Other species, large baits	Sizes 4 to 8, beak point, in-curved	Continental boilie
General feeder	Sizes 12 to 16, round bend	Carbon specimen
Feeder, strong fish	Sizes 12 to 16, beak point	Super spades
Feeder, roach, dace	Sizes 14 to 18, beak point	Super spades, ready tied
Float fish, flake hookbait	Sizes 8 to 12, crystal bend	Specimen crystal
Float fish, caster hookbait	Sizes 16 or 18, crystal bend	Carbon caster

Size 6 extra strong barbed treble hook

Size 8 extra strong barbed treble hook

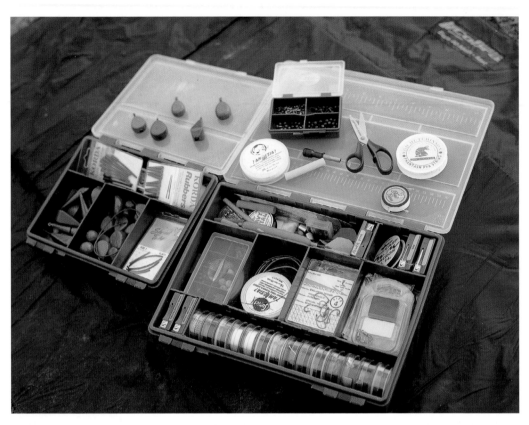

Lines

Modern monofilament lines are a vast improvement on those of even a few years ago. Diameter has decreased and breaking strains increased. Some of the new fluorocarbon lines are now virtually invisible in water.

Monofilaments

Whatever main line you use, there is one rule that applies at all times – change your lines regularly. All mono lines deteriorate in time, especially if continually exposed to the sun, and you should renew your lines at least three times a season.

The three monofilament main lines recommended are Drennan Specimen Plus, Berkeley Trilene XT and Sufix Synergy. Specimen Plus is the all-round main line in all breaking strains, but when you require greater abrasion resistance, the Trilene or Sufix lines are excellent.

All three lines are not ideal for hooklinks as they are a little springy. If you require a monofilament hooklink you need more limpness,

and then you might want to switch to Drennan Float Fish or Sufix Ultra Supreme. Anglers who fish for smaller fish will find their low diameters helpful in creating delicate bait presentation. One of the best standard pre-stretched lines with ultra-low diameter is Drennan Double Strength. One of the problems with extra-low diameter pre-stretched lines is that they tend to be a little stiff. A good compromise, if you require a little pre-stretch but a line that is ultra limp, is extra-soft Trilene XL or Pro Micron.

An exciting development in recent years has been the advent of fluorocarbon lines, which have the same refractive index as water. In other words, they become invisible on immersion. These enable very subtle bait presentations to be made, and the Sufix Invisiline is highly recommended if you are using monofilament links over 4 lb (1.81 kg) breaking strain.

ABOVE: Tackle boxes with compartments for lines, hooks, weights, leads and tools – essential for the serious angler.

Other Hooklink Materials

For most carp and barbel fishing soft braided hooklinks are suitable. Good braids are Drennan Carp Silk and Rod Hutchinson's The Edge. If you are fishing in woody snags, all braids can have a problem if the fibres are continually picked at by wood splinters, progressively weakening the material. Braids are also not ideal if fishing in heavy flows for chub and barbel, particularly upstream where the terminal tackle is constantly on the move, as they tangle very easily. In these situations, you may wish to revert to Drennan solid Dacron. Another alternative is a smoothly coated braid, of which there are many on the market.

Another specialized product from Rod Hutchinson is the Edge Plus, which is a braid with a fine lead core. Using several feet of this above the hooklink ensures that the main line is nailed to the bottom, thereby eliminating the problem of line bites. In barbel fishing, it also keeps the main line below drifting debris.

Super Braids

There is a growing use of ultra-low diameter, high-strength super braids. Many anglers are using these both as main lines and hooklinks, for the advantages of high strength-to-diameter ratio, zero stretch and good bait presentation. If you adopt this procedure, please be responsible. A 30 lb (13.6 kg) high-strength braid can be as fine as 7 lb (3.18 kg) mono, but a fish running into a snag could get tethered with no way of breaking free. These braids should really be reserved for hooklinks. This gives the advantage of enhanced bait presentation, but a main line break will still allow a hooked fish to escape.

There are two basic types of high-strength braid: round or flat section. However, some of the flat varieties are subject to sudden fracture if a wind knot develops. Some are also too stiff, although that does help to overcome the problem that occurs with all braids, that of tangling on the cast. The Sufix Herculine, available in breaking strains from 11 lb (5 kg) upwards, is recommended. This variety has a diameter roughly equivalent to 3 lb (1.36 kg) mono and makes a huge difference if you require fine presentation with a small hook for big powerful fish, such as feeder fishing for tench and barbel. The only problem with Herculine is that, because it is so limp, rigs must be as tangle proof as possible.

Trace Wires

It is a good idea to construct your own pike traces. Use 20 lb (9.07 kg) strand wire and simply twist the swivel and leading treble to the trace with at least a 1 in (2.5 cm) twist. A refinement is strand-coated wire, which is softer and limp to the touch. This is twisted in place in the same way and the plastic coating fused into a solid bond over a low flame. Whatever trace wire you use, make any pike trace at least 20 lb (9.07 kg) in strength and your traces at least 18 in (45 cm) long.

RIGHT: A fully equipped angler approaches the water in high summer. Much modern angling equipment is extremely light and sturdy compared to what was available just a few decades ago. The important thing during any fishing expedition is not to forget vital equipment, and running through a checklist before you set out is an excellent idea.

ABOVE: Just a few of the lines that are available in any tackle shop. Each one is clearly labelled with the purpose, diameter and breaking strain. Amnesia memory-free lines are being used more and more by all anglers whatever their quarry. The lines do not kink and are a great help in avoiding tangles.

Indicators

There are various ways that anglers go about registering when the fish has taken their bait. Some traditional indicators have been around for centuries; others, such as night floats and electronic alarms, are modern.

Floats

The most traditional bite indicators are floats, which exist in a myriad of different forms, in order to cope with various conditions and angling styles. As with all tackle, good products are available from several manufacturers.

Float design varies to cope with the fishing style involved, and generally those floats used for river work have their body bulk higher on the stem for stability of riding a current, while stillwater floats carry their bulk much lower to minimize the effects of drift. The table recommends float choices for various angling circumstances.

Type of Water	Example of Float
Gentle flow, small baits	Stick Float/Wire-stemmed Stick
All-round trotting in streamy water	Wire-stemmed Avon
Streamy water with large baits	Loafer or Crystal Avon
Fast, shallow runs through weed, large baits	Double-rubber Balsa
Short-range laying on, stillwaters or very gentle flow	Peacock Waggler
Short- to medium-range laying on, stillwaters	Insert Crystal Waggler
Long-range laying on, calm conditions	Crystal Missile
Medium- to long-range laying on, windy conditions	Driftbeater
Pike fishing, free-ranging livebait	Crystal Piker
Pike fishing, deadbait	E.T. Dumpy Slider
Pike fishing, driftbait	E.T. Drifter

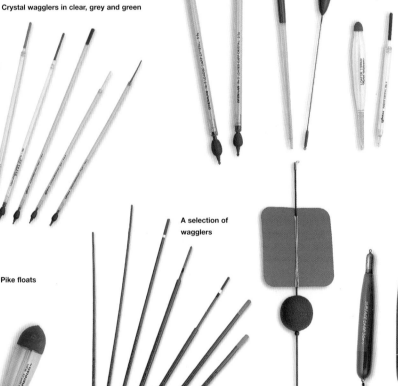

LEFT TO RIGHT: **Two loaded carp crystal floats, a stick float, a wire-stemmed stick float, a loafer and an inset crystal float.**

Crystal wagglers in clear, grey and green

A selection of wagglers

Pike floats

Drifting pike float

Wooden carp floats

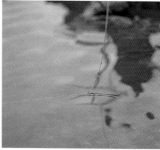

ABOVE: A quivertip set in its normal position. When a fish takes, the line will be pulled to the right.

LEFT: Electronic bite alarms coupled with bobbins.

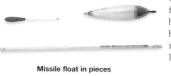

Missile float in pieces

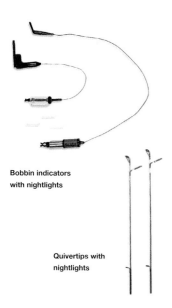

Bobbin indicators with nightlights

Quivertips with nightlights

Bobbins

The earliest form of legering incorporated a ball of dough hung on the line between the reel and the first rod ring to form an angle. A bite was signalled by the line tightening and the "dough bobbin"

rising. This term now includes any free-hanging bite indicator, which may be the top of a washing-up liquid bottle or sophisticated commercially made bobbins incorporating beta lights for night fishing.

Most anglers equip their bobbins with a retaining cord, tied to the rod rest, to prevent them being lost on a hard strike. The cord can be loaded with lead wire to make the bobbin heavier and counteract drift.

Butt Indicators

Butt indicators are pivoted arms set at the front rod rest, with the head of the indicator placed on the line a short distance in front of the reel. There are several types available.

The arm developed by Bob Henderson features a cleverly designed angled slot in the head, so that the indicator automatically falls away from the line when it reaches the horizontal. Many butt indicators have a problem of resistance to the line when they are pulled out of their retaining device. With the Henderson, the line falls away sweetly, totally resistance free.

For deadbait fishing for predators, when the reel is often fished free spool, butt indicators can be mounted on the rear rod rest, so that they rise and then pull off the line when a run starts. Recommended for fishing this style, are the droparm indicators or, for longer sessions, the E.T. Backbiter, which works on the same principle but incorporates the facility for including beta lights and provides an adjustable audible alarm.

Swingtips

As the name implies, a swingtip is a stiff extension to the rod tip, hinged to a threaded base to fit a matching threaded tip ring on the rod. Once the bait has been cast out, the line is tightened until there is the required angle in the swingtip. A bite is signalled by the tip either rising or falling. Swingtips can be fitted with lead wire to counteract drift, and beta lights for night work. They are mainly used in stillwaters or very sluggish sections of rivers.

Quivertips

Separate quivertips are either supplied with rods, spigotted or overfitted to the rod top after removing the tip ring, or supplied with threaded adapters to fit threaded tip rings. Unlike a swingtip, the thread is not hinged to the body, which is tapered to accentuate a bite from a fish. They are supplied in a range of test curves, from 3 oz (85 gm) for strong fish such as barbel to only 1 oz (28 gm) or less to indicate the bite from the most delicately feeding fish.

Electronic Alarms

Most anglers will be equipped with electronic alarms of one kind or another, usually in combination with bobbins or butt indicators, in order to give both visual and audible bite warning. The line is placed in the slot in the alarm head and a bite is then indicated with a bleep and flashing LED display when the line moves. There are many very reliable alarms available on the market.

ABOVE: A rucksack is a convenient way to carry all the equipment you need when you are out on a short expedition. Waterproof rucksacks keep all your equipment dry.

Luggage

You will need a special rucksack or probably a carryall to transport your equipment easily and safely. Rucksacks are suitable for the normal range of equipment, and a carryall is good for baits and flavours. An insulated bag is useful for frozen baits.

Rod Holdalls

There are four traditional holdalls available for carrying rods with reels attached. The Relum Logic Rod System takes up to five rod/reel assemblies on the outside, with an umbrella inside. External pockets accommodate rod rests, storm poles and landing nets. Separate sleeves can be purchased to accommodate up to 13 ft (3.96 m) two-piece rods, and the position of the reel pouches is adjustable.

Slings and Quivers

For the mobile angler, slings or quivers, in which one or two made-up rods are carried, together with a minimum of other bits and pieces, such as a landing net, rod rests and a lightweight umbrella, are a boon. Some slings have a quick-fasten retaining strap on the outside to keep made-up rods under control when on the move.

Carryall/Unhooking Mat

A useful item of luggage is the combined carryall/unhooking mat designed to carry a folding seat, plus items like buzzer bars, rod pods and bivvy; and when not in use, it opens out to make a good unhooking mat.

A large version has been made to accommodate the largest bedchair. For short fishing sessions, when you might just be carrying a rod and landing net, a large rucksack is not ideal, and in these circumstances a stalker bag may be preferable. This has four external and five internal pockets and sufficient room for the amount of gear and bait needed for a short session.

Ancillary Items

The list below is a general selection of useful items to include within your fishing equipment:

Range of leads from 0.25–3 oz (7–85 gm), container of split shot, range of floats.

Counterbalance and Flotsam, which are sinking and floating putty respectively.

Mini-night lights and screw-in beta light adapters.

Different strength screw in quivertips and swingtips.

Snap links, swivels and rig beads.

Hair rig needle and hair rig dumbbell stops.

Silicon tubing, for making semi-fixed bolt rigs and shrink tube.

Scissors, braid scissors, forceps and small screw-in scythe blade.

Polypops or cork balls, rig foam and superglue.

Line grease and a small bottle of washing-up liquid for degreasing.

Float and leger stops and float caps.

PVA string, tubes and bags.

Hook-sharpening stone plus small, sharp knife.

Rig, hooklink and licence wallets.

Headlamp torch, plus spare batteries and bulbs.

Camera, filters, spare films and batteries, cable release and air bulb for self portraits.

Insulating tape, rubber bands, Power Gum.

Bait droppers, catapults and Avon weighing scales.

Thermometer, notepad and pencil, small hand towel.

Syringe for air-injecting lobs.

First aid kit: including anti-allergy spray for insect bites and stings, headache tablets and suncream.

Mobile phone for emergencies.

BELOW: A special carryall designed to transport a number of rods and reels in safety.

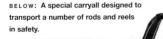

Ancillary Items

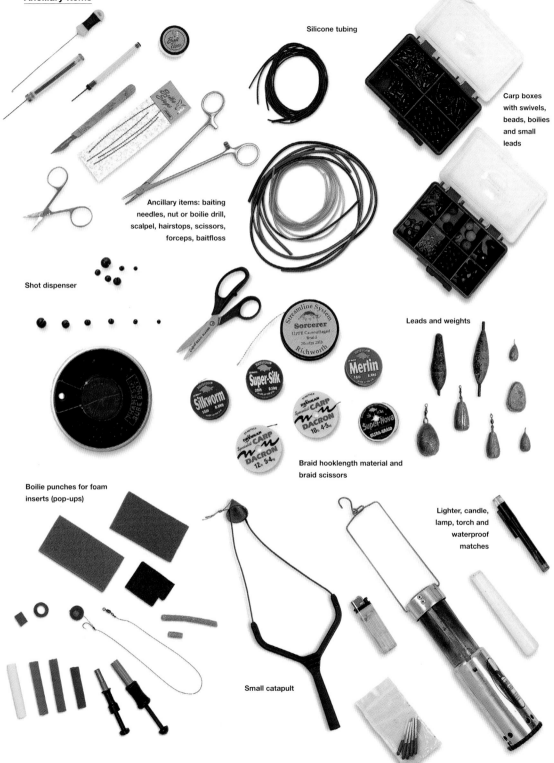

Silicone tubing

Carp boxes with swivels, beads, boilies and small leads

Ancillary items: baiting needles, nut or boilie drill, scalpel, hairstops, scissors, forceps, baitfloss

Shot dispenser

Leads and weights

Braid hooklength material and braid scissors

Boilie punches for foam inserts (pop-ups)

Lighter, candle, lamp, torch and waterproof matches

Small catapult

Float Fishing

Float fishing is one of the most popular coarse fishing methods. Whether it be studying intently for the tiniest knock as the float trots downstream, searching for roach, watching for those tell-tale rings to appear around the float at dawn on a tench lake, or starting in excitement as a drifting pike float disappears in a dramatic vortex, there is something almost mystical about the connection between float, bait, fish and fisherman.

Choosing a Float

Float fishing takes many forms, but all demand one constant factor to achieve the most efficient fishing. Always take the trouble to ensure that your choice of float is as suitable for the job in hand as possible, and that it is shotted correctly for maximum sensitivity. One of the most common mistakes beginners make is in struggling with a float that is far too light, particularly when trotting in running water. Do not try to convince yourself you are fishing more sensitively with too light a model – you will suffer poor presentation as a result. It is far better to use a float that is a little on the heavy side, and shot properly for perfect control.

The choice of floats is vast, both in type and manufacture, and can be very confusing for the novice. The all-

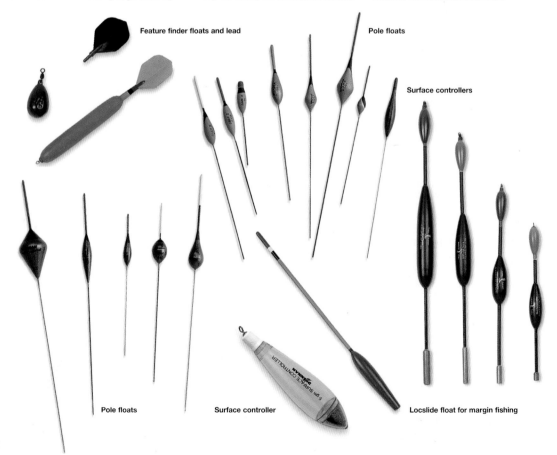

Feature finder floats and lead

Pole floats

Surface controllers

Pole floats

Surface controller

Locslide float for margin fishing

Trotting

ABOVE: A stick float on a correctly shotted line. A well-stocked shot dispenser is essential so extra shot can be added easily.

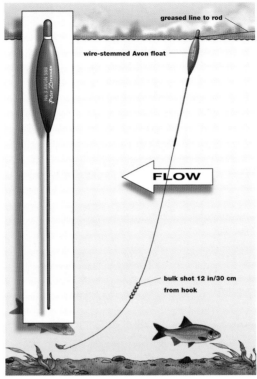

greased line to rod

wire-stemmed Avon float

FLOW

bulk shot 12 in/30 cm from hook

LEFT: A basic trotting rig for evenly paced water, presenting a bait near the bottom and showing the action of trotting a float downstream using an Avon float. The bait is lightly shotted, depending on the strength of the current, and drifts down naturally to the fish.

Check the depth of the swim, and see that the float moves easily without any unnatural drag or disturbance.

rounder will require, however, floats of many types, and it is best to build up your collection slowly, getting to know how each one behaves and in what circumstances it is best used.

The most important thing, whatever type of float fishing you are doing, is that the float must be clearly visible. This sounds obvious, but light conditions can vary so much that one day you may need a red- or orange-tipped float, but on the next day you may require black. Extreme variations can also occur on the same day. For this reason, those floats available with a range of interchangeable sight tips of different colours are invaluable. Insert crystals, where you can not only change the float-tip colour in an instant, but also alter the tip for a night-light just as quickly when darkness falls, are recommended.

Trotting

Trotting simply means running a float down the current, taking the bait to the fish, and is most applicable to long, uniform, gravelly glides. Other good swims for trotting are runs under high banks or fringing overhanging foliage, or creases, where you can work the float along the junction of the two flows. Swims under steep vertical banks containing undercuts, in times of high water, are great for

trotting. In these conditions all species pack into these undercuts. Fish the float right along the edge of the bank, holding it back hard at short intervals, so that the bait swings upwards and inwards to search under the undercut.

Although it is possible to trot with a normal fixed-spool reel, a much more efficient presentation is achieved with a smooth running centrepin or, in difficult winds, a closed-face reel. To keep as close a contact with the float as possible, the longest rod you can practically handle is advisable, but it needs to be light and responsive. For general trotting work, a 14 ft (4.27 m) rod is ideal.

Most trotting is carried out with Avon or Stick floats of various sizes, depending on the depth and speed of flow, the bait, the presentation required and species sought. For the beginner, the wire-stemmed Avon float is suitable. Control does not have to be exact, and it is not easily pulled off course. Apart from steady loose feeding – a dozen maggots or a pinch of mashed bread before each trot –

one important aspect of a good trotting presentation is the avoidance of drag, created by a sinking line between float and rod top.

It is advisable to ensure that the line floats before fishing. A spray-on silicone line floatant is recommended.

It is simple to lift surplus floating line off the water, to compensate for wind or current deviation and to keep direct contact with the float without disturbance. If the line sinks, keeping a tight line to the float can pull it off course or check it unnaturally, causing a wake, both of which make fish suspicious. Gently checking the float occasionally, providing it is not pulled off course, is a good way of inducing bites, as it makes the hookbait swing upwards in the water with the current.

Most fish will rise quite a way off the bottom to intercept a bait, and so you should set the float to just clear the bottom at the shallowest point of the swim. This is easily achieved by running the float through a few times to see where it drags.

Stret Pegging

Bigger-than-average specimens can sometimes be caught by searching those areas where some loose feed has settled out of the main flow. This is particularly true when you are trotting a swim bordered by much slower water, such as a crease. Periodically, it pays to push up the float, cast to the normal position and then let the float drift round on a tight line to settle in this slacker water. This laying on in streamy water is known as stret pegging.

It is necessary to use a rod rest while stret pegging, as the float is less prone to swing around than if the rod is held by hand, and false bites are therefore eliminated. The float will normally be fishing at half-cock when fished on a tight line in flowing water, but if it continually goes under because of water pressure, keep deepening the float setting to reduce the line angle and eventually it will settle in one place. If you find it impossible to prevent the float submerging, you are almost certainly fishing in too fast a flow, in which no bait would have settled anyway. It is important not to fall into the trap of increasing the float size and loading to cope with the fast flow, as you will then lose all control. Use the same tackle you used for trotting. If that float can be stret pegged properly, then you are fishing the slacker water.

One important point with stret pegging is that you are float fishing on a tight line, in a similar way to tight-line legering. This means that you could experience savage bites, particularly if your river contains big barbel or chub. Therefore, although you should use a rest, keep your hand on the rod butt just in case. Rods can fly into a river in these circumstances.

Stret pegging need not be completely static. Having thoroughly searched one area, say 5 yds (4.6 m) down from your sitting position, let

out some line and allow the float to trundle down a bit further. Close the bale arm and the float will resettle.

Try stret pegging at dusk. This is when the bigger fish move into the steadier water to feed, and you could well hook a bonus fish.

BELOW: Playing a good fish caught stret-pegging in the slacker water by the bush.

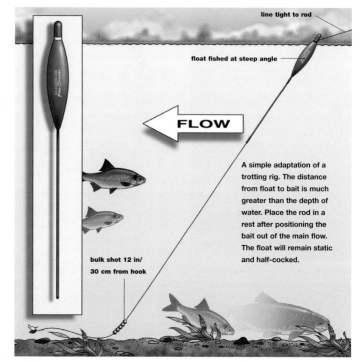

line tight to rod

float fished at steep angle

FLOW

A simple adaptation of a trotting rig. The distance from float to bait is much greater than the depth of water. Place the rod in a rest after positioning the bait out of the main flow. The float will remain static and half-cocked.

bulk shot 12 in/ 30 cm from hook

ABOVE: The diagram shows the effect of stret pegging, using the same tackle as for trotting (see page 71). Holding the float on a tight line pulls it half underwater, and the bait is held in one position. Fish move out of the streamy water and into the crease to feed. It is a good tactic to try in small streams like the one shown in the photograph below, and it is often surprising what large fish can be taken from relatively small waters.

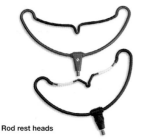

Rod rest heads

Laying On: Short Range

Laying On: Long Range

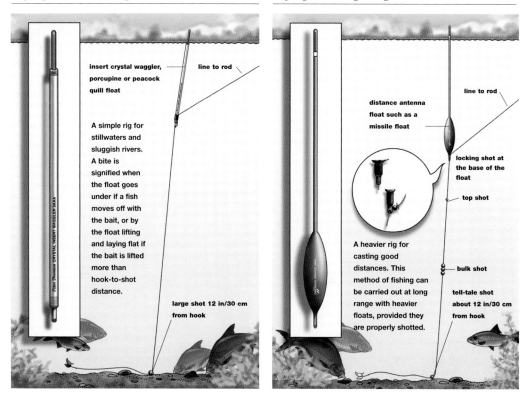

insert crystal waggler, porcupine or peacock quill float

line to rod

A simple rig for stillwaters and sluggish rivers. A bite is signified when the float goes under if a fish moves off with the bait, or by the float lifting and laying flat if the bait is lifted more than hook-to-shot distance.

large shot 12 in/30 cm from hook

distance antenna float such as a missile float

line to rod

locking shot at the base of the float

top shot

A heavier rig for casting good distances. This method of fishing can be carried out at long range with heavier floats, provided they are properly shotted.

bulk shot

tell-tale shot about 12 in/30 cm from hook

Laying On

Laying on is similar in concept to stret pegging, except that where the latter is carried out in streamy water, laying on is used in stillwaters or very sluggish flows. There is another important difference. As stret pegging is a tight-line technique, it is best used with an Avon-type float fixed top and bottom. For laying on, you generally wish to prevent drift so the float to use is a waggler type, fished bottom end only, with the line between float and rod top sunken.

The simplest form of laying on is with a quill float such as a peacock, cocked by one large shot about 12 in (30 cm) from the hook. The depth is set so that the distance from float to shot is slightly overdepth, and obviously the float will lie flat on a slack line. By placing the rod on a rest and slowly drawing the line tight, thereby creating an angle in the line, the float cocks. The tighter the line can be drawn, the lower and straighter the float becomes. This is then an ultra-sensitive set-up, the

ABOVE LEFT: Laying on: short range. The diagram illustrates the principle of laying on in stillwaters. The float is a waggler type and attached bottom end only. The float is cocked by drawing the line tight and the single shot rests on the bottom.

attentions of a fish becoming immediately apparent when this delicate balance is disturbed. The light loading means that this particular laying on is only suitable for short range, and at longer ranges you will need to employ heavier floats.

However, the general principle is the same for all laying on, which is that there is always between 6–24 in (15–60 cm) of line on the bed, so that bottom-feeding fish can take the bait without feeling any initial resistance.

Although you would normally lay on with the intervening line sunken, there is one instance when you would lay on with that line greased, and that is when fishing a bottom bait among dense lily pads. The foliage itself prevents drift, while the greased line resists sinking down between the

ABOVE RIGHT: Laying on: long range. Traditional laying on is for tench and bream. The bulk of the float buoyancy is counter-balanced by top and bottom shots so that bite registration is still indicated by the float going under or lifting when the shot moves.

lilies, inviting snagging. This type of laying on is deadly for stillwater tench and small stream perch.

Possibly the most traditional laying on is for tench and bream in over-grown estate lakes at dawn. Most anglers of a few years' experience will have experienced the sheet of tench bubbles rising around the float, before it starts to dither and tilt to the attentions of the fish. This is one of the exciting moments in angling and it is important to let the float go away before striking. If you continually miss bites it is possible you are striking too soon, so increase the distance from hook to bottom shot. If you are not seeing bites, but there are obviously fish active, shorten that distance. Trial and error will arrive at the right combination for the day.

Laying On: Lift Method – Short Range

Laying On: Lift Method – Long Range

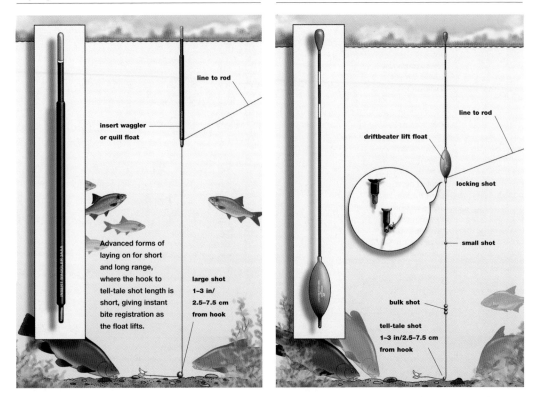

line to rod

insert waggler or quill float

Advanced forms of laying on for short and long range, where the hook to tell-tale shot length is short, giving instant bite registration as the float lifts.

large shot 1–3 in/ 2.5–7.5 cm from hook

driftbeater lift float

line to rod

locking shot

small shot

bulk shot

tell-tale shot 1–3 in/2.5–7.5 cm from hook

Lift Method

The lift method is a very precise method of laying on and is great for stillwater float fishing. The general principle is similar to laying on, except that the bottom shot is generally fished much closer to the hook than in pure laying on: 2–3 in (5–7.5 cm) from the hook is normal. Once the line has been drawn tight, it can be seen that when a fish picks up the bait, it will almost immediately take the weight of the shot. Released from its loading, the float will now try to lie flat by shooting up in the water, or "lifting". The closer to the hook this bottom shot is, the more sensitive is the method.

While the single shot set-up gives the most dramatic lifts, any waggler float can be arranged to promote very obvious bites. Having carefully loaded the float until it sits at perfect depth, with the all-important bottom shot close to the hook, carefully plumb the depth. Initially, the bottom shot should just be resting on the lake bed. The float will then be riding too high,

ABOVE LEFT: The depth is accurately plumbed and the single shot rests on the bottom. Any bite will lift the shot and the float will automatically "lift" to indicate the bite. Even the most delicate of bites will register. Use any waggler float, although a light quill that can be cocked with a single shot gives the most dramatic and exciting lift. Ideal for shy biting fish such as crucian carp.

therefore you should place the rod on a rest and draw the line tight as before, so that the float is fishing at its correct setting. The most delicate of bites will lift that bottom shot, with the result that the float rises.

There is nothing that restricts this method to close range or specially delicate presentations. Provided the tackle is balanced, very heavy floats can be employed. Long-range missiles, for instance, taking many swan shot to cock, are just as sensitive as tiny quills. The difference is that, as they are designed for long range, and you must be able to see the lift, it is usually necessary to have the bottom shot bigger in order to give a

ABOVE RIGHT: Again the depth is accurately plumbed and the bottom shot rests on the bed. Even if you need to fish at long range, provided the tackle is properly balanced, even the most delicate of bites will still register. One of the most exciting forms of this method is fishing at night for crucians with a night-light. As the float lifts a dark band appears in the water.

more exaggerated lift. The same principle applies to driftbeater floats, where the sight bob is merely a visual aid in rough weather.

Lift float fishing at night for crucians using an insert waggler fitted with a night-light is exciting. If the rig is fished with one shot, say a BB, 1 in (2.5 cm) from the hook, and plumbed exactly so that it only just touches bottom, and the night-light is flush with the surface, the most delicate crucian bite is immediately detectable. Even the tiniest lift is seen as a dark band appearing in the middle of the shaft of brightness, which of course is twice as long as the light because of its own reflection (see page 78).

Slider Float

When you wish to fish with a float at any depth at which casting a fixed float the required distance is impossible, you have to resort to a slider. Any float can be converted to a slider by making it free-running on the line and stopping it at the appropriate depth with a sliding stop knot and tiny bead.

Where a float has no bottom ring, an item of tackle called a swinger must be used. This was principally designed for very quick float changing to stop the need to break the tackle down completely, but is ideal also for use with the sliding float. The swinger is a fine length of silicon tubing force-fitted over a swivel, and the silicon itself adapts easily to a wide range of float stem thickness and then fits on to the bottom of the float.

To use the sliding float, shot the float as normal, with the float free-running, and leave the stop knot only a short distance above the float so that you can check its setting. When you are satisfied, wrap a piece of counterbalance putty around the bottom shot. Cast to the required spot, and then keep adjusting the depth setting until the float tip just peeps above the water. You now know that the bottom shot is just touching the bottom. Then make a note of the position of your stop knot on the line for future reference, remove the counterbalance putty, and you're ready to start fishing.

Sliding floats are also useful for pike fishing with free-roving livebaits or when trolling free rovers behind a boat. This generally involves the use of slim, cigar-shaped pike floats with the line through the centre. The most effective way to fish them is as sliders, using stop knots and beads. One benefit of this approach is that it allows simple depth adjustments between each drift and presentation, thereby thoroughly searching the water at all depths to find the feeding fish.

To tie a stop knot, take a short length of monofilament of lower breaking strain than the main line, for instance 6 lb (2.72 kg) breaking strain when fishing with 12 lb (5.44 kg) breaking strain for pike, fold it in half and lay it along the main line. You will now have created a loop in the finer line. Hold one of the tails to the main line, while wrapping the other

Fishing with a Slider Float

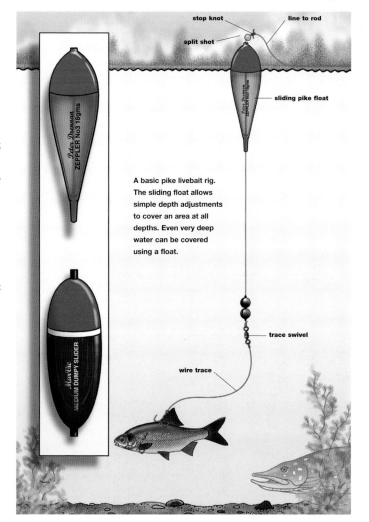

stop knot — line to rod

split shot

sliding pike float

A basic pike livebait rig. The sliding float allows simple depth adjustments to cover an area at all depths. Even very deep water can be covered using a float.

trace swivel

wire trace

ZEPPLER No3 18gms

MEDIUM DUMPY SLIDER

tail around the line four times and then passing it through the loop. Pull both tails tight, after first moistening the line to prevent excessive friction. Tighten until the knot slides only with difficulty, and you have it about right. Lastly, trim the tails to about ½ in (1 cm,) and there you have your sliding stop knot. Many anglers recommend using power gum stop knots but ordinarily monofilament is quite sufficient.

Continual adjustment of power gum knots can eventually cut through the material so that it falls off the line, at which point you have to start all over again.

ABOVE: This diagram shows one example of a sliding float to present a free-roving livebait for pike. This method of presentation can be used from the bank or from a boat, although as most pike live close to the reed beds around the margins of lakes, bank fishing is most common.

When fishing from a boat, the boat is allowed to drift with the wind, and the bait can be presented at various depths to search the water thoroughly for feeding fish.

The depth can be easily adjusted by moving the stop knot and bead up the line to increase the depth at which the bait is presented. The most normal presentation is as in laying on, when the bottom shot and bait are touching the bottom.

Float Legering

A specialized form of laying on is float legering, where the bottom shot is replaced by a standard leger weight. In this technique, the float is shotted so that it rides at its correct position, but is also anchored to the bottom to prevent drifting. The setting makes it very rare to get any bite indication other than a sudden disappearance of the float, as a fish takes line through the leger-weight swivel.

Float legering does not enjoy tremendous popularity now that very efficient butt indication systems are available, but it is worth considering in those circumstances where it still has great advantages.

The first is in medium- to long-range float fishing in very rough conditions where even a driftbeater lift float cannot cope with the undertow. These conditions are more easily tackled with conventional leger tactics, but if you gain more enjoyment from watching a float, then this is a situation that suits float leger tactics.

The second circumstance is if you need to fish over wide weed margins. A good approach is to grease the line from float to rod to prevent it sinking into the foliage. This, though, can lead to severe drift problems with normal float fishing and the float leger is the ideal solution.

The third most common use is in predator fishing with legered deadbaits or paternostered livebaits off the bottom, especially from a boat. The paternoster is explained in the section on legering (page 91).

Pike and zander anglers wish to avoid one thing above all others: deep hooking. It can sometimes be difficult to know when to strike a pike run on leger tactics; in fact from a boat the motion of the waves can make bite detection difficult. The float leger solves that, as the only reason for the float to go under is the attentions of a pike. The float-paternostered livebait is also a good tactic for pike fishing in fast-flowing rivers, where a dragging paternoster link slows down the rate of progression of the bait downstream.

There are several waters that actually have bans on straightforward legering; most of these waters have dense weed or lily-bed margins that have led to bad angling practices in the past, for example the use of excessively strong lines to drag fish through the undergrowth thereby causing damage. The famous tench water, Sywell Reservoir, falls into this category and the float leger is now the standard tactic among Sywell angling regulars.

Float Leger: Wide Reed Margins

Float Leger: Deadbait Fishing for Pike

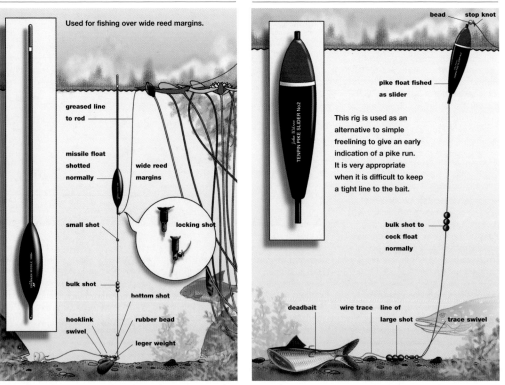

ABOVE: The float leger fished over wide reed margins. It is important to grease the line so that it does not sink as this would undoubtedly snag. The angler must ensure that the bottom lead is set at the correct depth and this may require trial and error to cope with the reed margin.

ABOVE: A traditional use for the float leger is when deadbait fishing for pike. The weight of the bait helps to anchor it to the bottom, preventing drift and the first indication the angler has of a bite is when the float disappears. This is a good rig when boat fishing.

Float Leger: Paternoster for Pike

stop knot — bead

pike float fished
as slider

A basic
paternoster rig
for presenting an
off-bottom bait.
This rig is for pike
but is also
effective for
zander.

swivel

snap link
trace swivel
wire trace

John Wilson
TENPIN PIKE SLIDER No2

lead link of lower breaking
strain than
mainline
leger weight

Float Leger: Pike Paternoster for Rivers

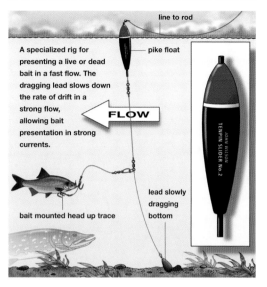

line to rod

A specialized rig for
presenting a live or dead
bait in a fast flow. The
dragging lead slows down
the rate of drift in a
strong flow,
allowing bait
presentation in strong
currents.

pike float

FLOW

lead slowly
dragging
bottom

bait mounted head up trace

JOHN WILSON
TENPIN SLIDER No.2

ABOVE: This is the same principle as the left diagram. The leger weight
slows down the progress of the livebait as it is carried downstream,
giving the pike more time to strike.

LEFT: Using this rig avoids the pike taking the bait right down and
prevents deep hooking as the angler can safely strike when the float
disappears. By substituting normal hooklink and normal baits, it can be
used to present static off-bottom bait for all coarse fish. The float is
used to keep the line taut.

Float Feeder

A natural progression from float
legering is float-feeder fishing, in
which the leger weight is replaced by
a swimfeeder, thereby ensuring
continual topping up of the loose feed
around the hookbait. The normal way
to feed when float fishing is to place
balls of groundbait around the float
periodically, or catapult quantities of
particles, or both. When fishing at
longer ranges, loose feeding with free
particles becomes impossible, and you
then have to rely on balls of
groundbait containing whatever
particles you are using.

The longer the range you fish, the
more problems you will have with
baiting accuracy, and in this
circumstance the float feeder is
appropriate. At least you can be
certain that there will always be feed
around the hook bait, whatever your
casting accuracy. You should still aim
to fish the same area consistently for
maximum angling efficiency, but
even the best anglers and finest

casters cannot hope to hit exactly the
same spot every time at 60 yds (55 m)
in a crosswind.

Why bother with a float in the first
place when it would be simpler to
revert to standard feeder tactics,
which in 99 per cent of cases would
be the most sensible course of action?
Many anglers do not enjoy their
fishing without a float to watch, and
this is a method that unites the
feeding benefits of the swimfeeder
with the aesthetic pleasure of
watching the float. The float feeder,
using very small feeders, is a popular
tactic at long range, especially on
bream waters where accurate baiting
of each cast is very important.

The most obvious use of the float
feeder, however, is in fishing over
wide weed or lily margins, in the
same way as for the float leger. Again,
straightforward feeder fishing may
create tremendous problems as the
weed inevitably wraps itself round
large lengths of sunken line. The float
feeder avoids this.

Float Feeder Rig

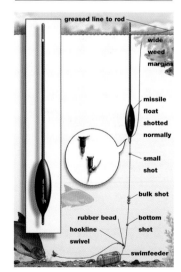

greased line to rod

wide
weed
margins

missile
float

shotted
normally

small
shot

bulk shot

rubber bead
hookline
swivel

bottom
shot

swimfeeder

ABOVE: An alternative to legering using a
swimfeeder that minimizes snagging.

Drift Float

On large stillwaters, normal methods of pike fishing limit the angler to about 80 yds (73 m) from the bank unless a boat is available, and considerably less if you are fishing with a livebait. To be able to fish beyond these limits demands the use of special drift floats designed both to catch the wind and to be visible at long range. The superb E.T. models fold flat during the retrieve, thereby presenting minimal water resistance, and are highly recommended.

As you can effectively fish the drift at ranges up to 200 yds (183 m) you need a large capacity fixed-spool reel loaded with a minimum of 12 lb (5.44 kg) line, which must be well greased. A long length of sunken line is going to present tremendous problems with drag. A useful piece of kit is an autogreaser, a rubber ring packed with grease that fits the butt ring. Fishing the drift float for pike demands great concentration at all times, because no other method of piking carries with it a greater risk of deep hooking. As soon as the float disappears, tighten down immediately, and set the hooks with a long sustained pull, walking backwards if possible. A normal strike is ineffective at such long range.

One of the real advantages of drift-float fishing is that it allows very thorough searching of a water at all ranges and depths. By progressively deepening the float setting between drifts, you can automatically locate hot spots such as gravel bars, as the float will stop drifting as it reaches the obstacle. As all predators love to hide behind such features, it is a good idea to search these areas thoroughly. The ideal weather conditions are a moderate to fresh breeze, which allows efficient drifting without the speed of drift being uncontrollable. Good drift floats will set lower in the water for more stability when there is a good wind and higher when you need to catch as much of a light breeze as possible.

The problem with drift-float fishing in very light winds is that, having located a hot spot well offshore, it can be a frustratingly slow business getting another bait out there, especially if the wind changes direction quickly.

A livebait being retrieved long distances will quickly tire if it is attached to the trebles in the normal way – with the top treble attached below the dorsal and the lower treble in the top lip – as it will be retrieved against water pressure side on. If you are fishing with a drift float and a livebait, mount your livebaits head up the trace, as it is far easier on them during the retrieve.

Drift Float

Night Float

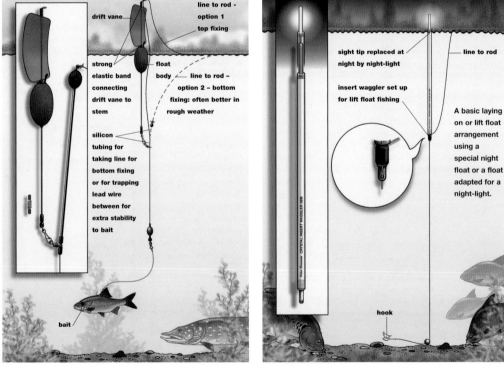

ABOVE: A specialized technique for taking pike at ultra-long range in large stillwaters. It demands constantly greased line to work effectively and the wind behind you.

ABOVE: An excellent rig for night fishing for crucian carp, bream, carp and roach. When a fish bites the float lifts and a dark band appears in the circle of light cast by the float.

Casting a Waggler Float

Fishing with a waggler float is a favourite method for many anglers and is commonly used on many stillwaters when fishing for roach, tench, carp and other species. The waggler is cast in an overhead manner, after which the line between the rod and the waggler is sunk beneath the surface of the water. This eliminates any drag on the float and enables it to hold its position. Once the float has settled in the water, the angler places the rod in the rod rest. When a fish bites and the float is drawn under, the angler picks up the rod and is into the fish. The tip of the waggler can be used as a marker at which to fire groundbait.

This photographic sequence shows the angler making the cast, after which the rod is placed in the rod rest and groundbaiting can begin.

1 The bale arm of the reel is opened to allow the line to run free. The line is trapped under a finger.

2 The rod is swept back over the head of the angler and then forward in one movement.

3 The float flies out towards the water and as it hits the water the angler slows down the line by cushioning the spool of the reel with his finger to act as a brake.

4 The bale arm of the reel is now engaged and the tip of the rod dipped under the surface. Two or three turns are wound on to the reel making the line sink under the water.

5 The rod is placed on the rod rest with the tip just under the surface. Should the angler have to react to a bite all he has to do is pick up the rod and connect with the fish.

6 Once the rod is safely in the rod rest the angler can start to catapult feed out towards the float. The tip of the float acts as a marker for the angler to aim at.

Casting and Striking with a Swimfeeder

Feeder fishing is a good way to catch bigger fish, especially bream, and uses a swimfeeder instead of a lead. The feeder is filled with groundbait and a few maggots and then cast to a mark in front of the angler. The feed inside will soon disperse, once the feeder has reached the bottom of the water. If the angler casts to the same spot each time, eventually fish will be drawn to the swim. When the fish settle on the feed, the angler will start to catch them as they pick up the hookbait near the free offering of food.

This is a good method for bream. When hooked, play bream carefully as they are slow, dogged fighters, and if you are too hard on them they may throw the hook.

1 Fill the swimfeeder and then pick a mark on the far bank to aim at. Open the bale arm on the reel and face the front looking at the mark.

2 Swing the rod back and when the feeder is extended behind, start the forward drive. Release the line so that it runs off the reel.

3 The rod is driven forward with the right hand and the left hand pulls the butt downwards to accelerate the progress of the cast.

4 As the swimfeeder and bait reach the water the angler cushions the spool with his forefinger to slow it down. The bale arm is still open.

5 When the feeder hits the bottom the rod tip falls back. Close the bale arm, bring the rod sideways and wind in until the rod has a slight curve.

ABOVE: A full moon rises on the water of a small lake. Fishing at night is full of surprises with strange noises and night creatures.

6 The angler places the rod in the rest and sits at a 45-degree angle as this will enable him to detect a bite from a fish. The soft-actioned rod tip will either be drawn forward or drop back slightly. The angler will strike if he sees either of these movements. Bigger bream tend to take the rod tip around in a slow, forward movement, giving plenty of time for the angler to connect with the bite.

7 When he sees a bite the angler raises the rod and strikes in a gentle manner. Smaller bream, called skimmers, will be lost if the strike is too hard. As the strike is made, the angler watches the rod and feels the fish to gauge how large it is.

This fish is hooked and all that remains is for it to be brought to the net. Take care and do not be too hard on bream as they are easily lost.

Freelining

The simplest approach to angling is to have a hook and bait on the line and nothing else and, where possible, this is one of the most natural presentations you can make. Virtually every coarse fish can, at times, be pursued effectively using freelining tactics, from a single maggot on gossamer tackle trundling downstream towards a big dace over gravel shallows, or a chunk of liver fished in the margins for a giant catfish.

When to Use Freelining

True freelining is where the tackle is totally weightless, and therefore only certain conditions are suitable. For visual bite detection you have to rely on either watching the fish take the bait or seeing the line move, and if there is much wind the technique becomes difficult to apply and therefore ineffective.

Where you are freelining big baits for big fish in stillwaters, say large deadbaits for pike or catfish, you usually get decent runs, but even in these situations a good wind could force you to use some lead, so that you can tighten to the bait properly.

The most effective bite detection method for freelining in rivers is undoubtedly feeling the bites with your fingers, especially where there is a decent flow to tighten the line naturally. Obviously, there will be a certain speed of flow where you will need to add lead, but where this can be avoided you can fish very delicately. Freelining slow-sinking flake over gravel shallows for chub, especially fishing upstream, allows the bait to bump back down towards you. Bouncing meat through a summer streamer bed for barbel is also an ideal freelining situation.

Stalking

Mobile stalking with natural baits is exciting fishing, especially on over-grown waters where your hunting instincts can come to the fore. Natural baits taken by fish include small fish, frogs, caterpillars, crayfish, and even young waterfowl. However, worms and slugs are the most common baits taken by fish and used by anglers.

The most important aspect of successful stalking is a stealthy approach. If you have managed to get within casting range of fish, say chub in a clearing in a rush bed, or carp in dense lilies, without their being aware of your presence, and you are capable of a half-decent cast, there is no reason why the bait should not be taken instantly. All fish are opportunist feeders, and do not pass up the chance of a free meal if they have no reason to be alarmed.

Consider a large carp in the margins rooting around in the silt. This is a fish obviously feeding and searching for natural baits, an ideal situation for the presentation of free-lined lobworm or a bunch of redworms. If you have not spooked the fish on the cast, be prepared for what happens next, because it is very common for the carp to engulf the bait at top speed. You must be prepared for this potentially violent reaction by not having the line too tight, as this will result in a devastating smash and a badly spooked fish. Always allow a little slack to give the carp some time to turn with the bait before you strike.

Sometimes, even if fish are not obviously perturbed by the bait's sudden appearance, they appear to treat it with indifference and, in these circumstances, they need inducement to take your bait. This is particularly true of a chub. It can lie looking at the bait, totally disinterested, but suddenly pull it away and he pounces on it. Like a kitten with a ball of wool, it is an instinctive reaction.

A favourite example of stalking is fishing gravel shallows at dawn for big perch, using minnows or bleak. At this time of day, perch are voracious and very catchable from shallow water if you can keep quiet. Even though you may pinch a swan shot on the line when fishing minnow, it is still essentially freelining, and the bait is cast to the upstream end of the shallows and allowed to bump down with the flow. Takes can be savage, and you must stay alert and be prepared to give a little slack before striking. You may only retrieve the head of the minnow if you have the line too tight.

LEFT: An angler at his ease sits and lets the bait drop downstream in a fast-running weir pool. This is an excellent place to try freelining tactics.

Dense Baits

In high summer, many fish will be found lying in tiny gaps in foliage, and most of these swims will demand the use of totally static baits to prevent constant snagging. Natural baits such as slugs are nowhere near as effective here, as they are better fished on the move. For true static ambush baits in dense foliage, a heavy snag-resistant bait that hits the bottom quickly is ideal, and offerings such as cheese paste, luncheon meat or boilies can be more effective than naturals.

The swims that most require the use of dense-bait freelining are streamer weed beds, where the clear areas between the tresses are so narrow you need to be sure the bait sinks where it is cast. At first glance, a stretch of summer river apparently choked with ranunculus looks daunting, if not impossible, but 40 yds (36.6 m) of streamer weed can contain dozens of little clear runs, and each one can harbour fish, particularly chub, barbel and roach. Accurate casting is essential for successful freelining in streamer weed. The bait has to land in the clear water and sink

naturally. If it alights on top of the weed itself and drags, you have blown your chances in that swim. Casting accuracy is easier with a heavier bait, and if chub or barbel are the quarry, a good lump of cheese paste or luncheon meat is ideal. Fish lying under streamer weed take baits with great confidence as long as they arrive in a natural fashion, and large catches of summer fish are possible.

Apart from streamer beds, any densely overgrown area can often only be fished freelining heavy baits, and it is an undeniable fact that big fish of many species and dense snags go together. In such areas, rarely will you have the luxury of playing fish in the accepted sense of the word. The only option is one of hook and hold, for which adequate tackle is essential. You are well advised to step up your normal gear in these situations. For instance, a standard main line for carp fishing would be 12 lb (5.44 kg), but for short range stalking in snags 18 lb (8.16 kg) may be necessary. Strong hooks that will not pull out under extreme pressure are a must.

Deadbait

For really big pike, one of the most reliable methods is freelining large static deadbaits such as half a mackerel, herrings, or an eel section. These baits are dense enough to cast a fair distance without lead, but casting distance will be enhanced by using frozen baits. For a half mackerel, trim the tail fin and section the body at an angle, thus maximizing casting range. It goes without saying that you should freeze your baits individually and make sure they are straight. It is no fun on a freezing winter morning trying to unravel a whole block of frozen fish, and it's impossible to cast a herring shaped like a banana far.

You must utilize efficient bite registration when freelining for pike, in order to avoid a deeply hooked fish. It is therefore important to take in all the slack before attaching a drop-off pike indicator so you get instant warning of a pick-up. Make sure your indicator has enough weight to show drop-back bites. Very light arms may stay in place as the line is falling slack while a pike comes towards the bank with the bait. If wind or drift makes it difficult to tighten properly then you

should use a little lead or a float. That bite must be seen immediately.

When freelining large deadbaits, a 20 lb (9.07 kg) wire trace at least 2 ft (60 cm) long carrying two treble hooks, in sizes 6 or 8, are suitable. The point of the upper treble is inserted firmly in the tail root, while the lower treble is nicked as lightly as possible along the bait's flank.

For really tough-skinned baits, especially eel section, you can have problems pulling out of the bait and into the pike. You can either pare away a section of skin where the treble point is to go and then lightly hook into the flesh itself or, for long casting, nick the skin as lightly as possible and hold the trace in place for the cast by a tie of PVA string. It is a matter of personal preference whether you use barbless trebles or not; some anglers swear by them, while others have lost too many pike for their liking using them.

Whatever hooks you use, strike pike runs immediately and be properly equipped to unhook the pike quickly and without damage. Use wire cutters to snip off the barbs.

Making a Deadbait Trace for Pike

1 You will need: 20 lb (9.07 kg) seven strand wire; size 6 semi-barbless hooks; forceps; a twizzle stick; wire cutters; swivel; bomb weight with a large size 12 swivel; crimps; a pair of pliers; bore-run ring; an oval or rubber bead and bait.

5 Now thread on the second treble hook and move it down the trace until it is within 7 in (18 cm) of the bottom treble.

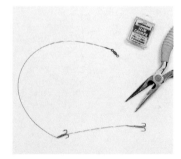

9 Thread the crimp on to the trace, followed by the swivel. Now take the end of the wire back down through the crimp, trapping the swivel in the process. Pull the crimp tight to the eye of the swivel and crimp it in position using a pair of pliers.

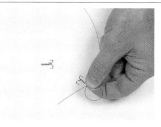

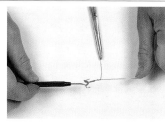

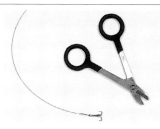

2 Cut a 20 in (50 cm) length of wire and thread a treble hook on to it at one end. Take the wire back through the eye of the hook, so the treble is now caught in a loop of wire.

3 Pull the tag end of the wire tight, trapping the hook. Then take the tag end in the forceps. Holding the hook in the twizzle stick, spin the forceps around the main wire trace.

4 Make sure the wire is twisted tightly in place and the hook is secure. Trim any remaining tag with wire cutters. This will not need crimping as twisting is sufficient.

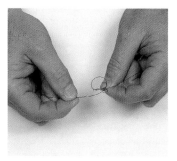

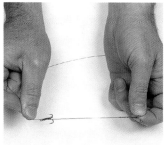

6 Bring the loose end of the trace around and under the treble hook so the wire is caught between the joint of the points on the treble. Pull the wire tight.

7 Start to wind the loose end of the wire back around the shank of the treble. At the top of the shank, take the wire up through the eye of the hook and pull it tight.

8 The second hook should now be held tightly in place by the wire trace. All that remains to be done is to crimp into position a size 12 swivel at the other end of the trace.

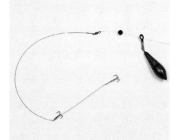

10 With the trace complete, it is time to connect it to the mainline. Take the mainline from the rod tip and thread on a swivel bomb fitted with a large bore run-ring. The run-ring allows line to pass through it with minimal resistance when a pike picks up the bait. Thread on a bead; this acts as a shock stop for the lead. Take the mainline and tie it to the swivel with a five-turn blood knot.

11 With the rig tied up and ready to fish, all you need to do is add a bait. A whole mackerel can be used to good effect as a deadbait when seeking out pike. Take the top treble and push one of the hook points into the stem bone of the tail. The second treble is inserted into the flank of the mackerel. The bait is then cast out and the wait for a take begins.

Surface Fishing

Most species of coarse fish at some time or another will take baits off the surface, and this provides some of the most exciting visual angling there is. The surface-feeding behaviour of fish such as chub, rudd and carp is well known, but not so well known is that predators like pike, perch, catfish, eels and zander will take baits off the top. Even those bottom-feeding stalwarts, tench and barbel, occasionally behave in this manner, although this is rare.

Both stillwaters and rivers vary as to whether they are good surface-fishing venues or not, sometimes for no apparent reason. A general rule of thumb in rivers is depth; the shallower, more intimate venues are more prone to surface-feeding behaviour than deep, powerfully flowing stretches. This is no great mystery as fish in shallow waters are more likely to come into contact with surface food items on a regular basis.

Chub will be used to moths under trees, and roach and dace to small

ABOVE: A big carp taking a piece of bread flake from the surface. Be prepared for the first run when the fish is hooked.

BELOW: Carp cruising on the surface on an estate lake. Good carp can very often be caught on a floating bait.

flies on the shallows. Narrow rivers are more likely to be overhung with foliage, especially in summer, and this leads to all manner of bugs, beetles and berries falling in to enhance the piscine larder beneath.

Although small intimate stillwaters often exhibit reliable surface feeding for similar reasons, there is no doubt that some waters are just not worth fishing off the top, while in others it is a deadly method. A famous example of this is the Redmire Pool, near Ross-on-Wye in Herefordshire. Although no one can deny that this is small,

overgrown and intimate, in fact it has always been a very poor surface water. Of all fish, carp are one of the happiest taking surface baits, but the Redmire carp are very reticent.

With all varieties of surface fishing, except anchored techniques, the most important thing is to make sure the line between bait and rod top floats, otherwise long lengths of sunken line make any attempt at a natural presentation virtually impossible. Bear in mind the alternatives of line grease or silicone spray floatant, available in aerosol cans.

Running Water

There are certain river swims where floating baits are particularly effective. These are usually shallow, gravelly runs with a lively current, especially where the current starts to slow as the depth increases. These shallows often hold large numbers of fish in summer, as they are naturally high in oxygen.

The most reliable surface-feeder in rivers is the chub, and the most basic bait is bread crust. Although allowing a chunk of crust to drift naturally with the flow is simple in concept, there are important considerations to avoid becoming frustrated with the technique. Natural bait presentation is vital. The crust must be free to follow all current variations, without moving unnaturally across the flow or, worse still, dragging and causing a wake. It requires practice to learn how much line to let out as the crust progresses downstream. Too little, too slowly, will result in drag, while too much will see loops of line on the surface drifting everywhere, possibly even pulling the crust off course, particularly on a windy day.

Other surface baits are often more effective for chub, especially when they have become spooked on crust after one or two have been taken on it. Items like dog biscuits, floating cereals or feed pellets can be used in

Pet-food mixer

Carp hook
and pellets

Surface controllers

sufficient quantities to initiate preoccupied surface feeding, and this largely overcomes the chub's natural caution. Floating boilies also make superb chub baits.

Pet-food mixers and trout pellets are also very effective chub baits. They are the right size, visible at range, and remain buoyant for a long time. If you cannot obtain bait bands, trout pellets and pet-food mixers can be superglued to the back of the hook

shank. For surface fishing, the floating putty, known as flotsam, is good. A small rough piece attached to the line resembles a piece of bark and floats like cork. Attach flotsam approximately 18 in (45 cm) from the hook and it will serve both as an extra flotation aid and a sight bob, the latter being more important with small baits like trout or koi pellets, which can become extremely difficult to see at long range.

A string of floating boilies

BELOW: A fast-running shallow on an overgrown stream. This type of water is ideal for surface fishing.

Calm and Stillwaters:
Fishing at Close Range

On quiet, overgrown river stretches, where a more orthodox approach is impossible, dapping is a method of fishing for chub in which you arrange for a natural bait to rest just on the surface film, with no surplus line to cause alarm. It is a particularly good method to use under overhanging trees, where the chub become used to insects of all types falling into the water. You can use deadbaits such as moths and caterpillars and impart life to them by gently twitching the line.

A similar process is fishing the margins of stillwaters for carp with crust. There the angler sits well back from the water's edge so that the rod just protrudes from the bankside cover. Slowly lower the baited hook so that it just breaks the surface film, and then stay alert, with slack line in your hand. Takes can be sudden and violent and these forms of close-range surface fishing are very exciting indeed. As this fishing will usually be close to snags, it pays to step up the gear, but this is not detrimental as no line will be on the surface anyway, the bait being all the fish sees.

Away from the margins of stillwaters, unfettered surface baits are still viable, but the further out you wish to fish, the more casting weight you will require and the more troublesome any wind will become. An exception to this may be among dense lily pads, where the pads themselves both act as a brake against wind action and help to disguise the line. Good casting weight is provided by high-protein floaters which, despite being buoyant, are quite dense. A terrific presentation is to hold a chunk of floater or crust hard against a lily pad with the line over it, which then looks completely natural.

Totally unfettered baits can also be used at greater range in stillwaters, taking advantage of any offshore breeze by drifting baits down the wind lanes. As with fishing rivers with trout pellets for chub, the longer you spend prebaiting these wind lanes with free offerings, say for carp or rudd, the greater will be the chances of success when they are followed by a hook bait. One ploy to use when surface fishing for carp in this way, when a good breeze is blowing across a bay and the windward bank has dense

rushy margins, is drifting freebies down wind. These will then pile up against the rushes leading, eventually to a good number of carp feeding there furiously.

In exactly the same way as river fishing, this drifting of freebies demands the use of greased line to fish properly. Carp will not tolerate any unnatural movement of the bait.

Drifting Stillwaters

If you want to fish a stillwater at long range with small, lightweight baits such as cereals, dog biscuits and trout pellets, extra casting weight is required to make the tackle controllable, and some form of visual bite indication is needed. The simplest addition is a small self-cocking float, and this is the choice if you are simply drifting baits down wind lanes. Where much more casting weight is required, say for reaching a group of carp basking alongside lilies 50 yds (46 m) away, or a shoal of rudd priming well offshore, you will need to substitute the relatively light float for a floating carp bomb or controller. In essence this is a floating leger weight. With a controller, it is possible

to fish just as effectively on the surface as it is legering at the same distance, although obviously it is more difficult to maintain as direct a contact. Keep the controller about 30 in (76 cm) from the bait, and keep the line well greased.

One of the main problems with the method is false bites, or coming short, caused by fish spooking at the sight or feel of the hooklink. This can be tremendously frustrating when fishing for big carp, especially if a couple of fish have already been taken using this method.

An ingenious way round the problem is to use what is known as a suspender rig, designed to keep all but the bait off the water, even at long range. To make a suspender, take about 18 in (45 cm) of thin rigid rig tubing, and then glue a large polyball about a third from one end. Closer to the same end of the tubing, wrap lead wire until, when testing in a bath of water, it floats tilted at about 45 degrees. For fishing the suspender, run the line through the weighted end first and attach hook and bait. At this point you need to take care that the rig is exactly the right distance from

Controller Used for Floating Bait

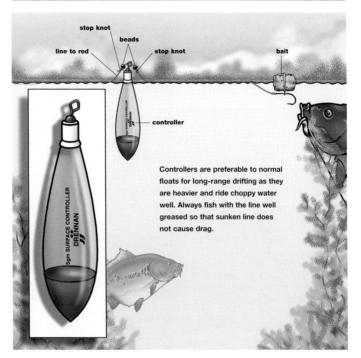

Controllers are preferable to normal floats for long-range drifting as they are heavier and ride choppy water well. Always fish with the line well greased so that sunken line does not cause drag.

Suspender Rig for Stillwater Drifting

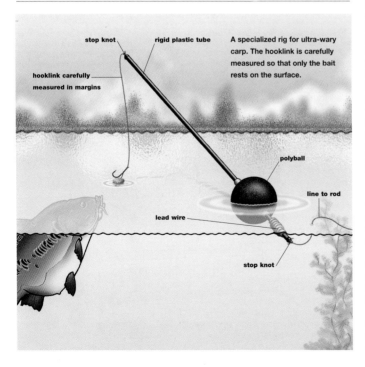

A specialized rig for ultra-wary carp. The hooklink is carefully measured so that only the bait rests on the surface.

the hook, as you want the bait to just rest on the surface; experiment in the margins to get this exactly right. When it is correct, place power gum stop knots at each end of the rig in order to keep it fixed. Hook-to-rig distance must be measured very accurately. If it is too long, line could lie round the bait in coils, destroying the whole purpose of the rig. If it is too short, a very light bait could actually hang clear of the water. When fishing the suspender, bites are very obvious and often very savage. The tilted tubing is highly visible, and really slaps down in the water when you get a take.

TOP: A floating bait with a controller. This enables the angler to present a floating bait to fish a considerable distance away in stillwater. The line needs to be well greased.

LEFT: A suspender rig is an ingenious device designed to keep everything off the water except the bait. It can be difficult to achieve the correct distance between hook and rig.

OPPOSITE: Surface fishing for carp feeding close-in on a still stretch of river. This can be one of the most exciting forms of angling.

Anchored Baits

When you wish to present a surface bait to carp or rudd out of normal casting range, and there is so much wind or drift that you find it impossible to keep the bait where it is required, the anchored floater rig provides the solution. It is fished with a heavy lead of at least 2 oz (57 g), connected to a large diameter plastic ring, or floater loop, by a length of line that is lighter than the main line.

Having cast into position, leave the pick-up open to allow the bait to rise to the surface, which it does easily through the low-friction floater loop. Close the pick-up, take in the slack and wait for the bite. You will find that floating baits like chunks of crust or high-protein floater rise easily, whereas for items like pet-food mixers even the small amount of friction and line drag can hold the bait down below the surface. For these baits, it is advisable to doctor the hook with a little rig foam to increase its buoyancy. For bite detection, as it is essentially a tight line-legering technique, normal butt indication systems are ideal.

One of the major problems with all surface fishing, particularly with baits such as bread crust, is the attention of birds, both of water and air. This is where anchored methods have a slight edge. By taking in 1 ft (30 cm) of extra line, the bait can actually be fished just below the surface. This is still perfectly acceptable to the fish but not quite as obvious to passing feathered traffic, especially if there is a nice ripple. Obviously, birds will eventually find it, but the delay gives the fish you are seeking that much longer to get in first.

The deeper the water, and the weedier the bottom, the more difficult it becomes to fish the rig properly, and you need to use the longest bomb link possible, say with a free-running balsa float body to keep it up, so that the hooklink has the minimum distance to travel before breaking the surface. As it is obviously difficult to cast out with a 15 ft (4.6 m) lead link in place, you need to coil it carefully and tie it in place with PVA ties. As the PVA dissolves in water after the cast, the balsa takes the link to its full extension. The major problem with this set-up comes when playing a fish, as you now have a 15 ft (4.6 m) lead link swinging around, which is

The Anchored Floating Bait

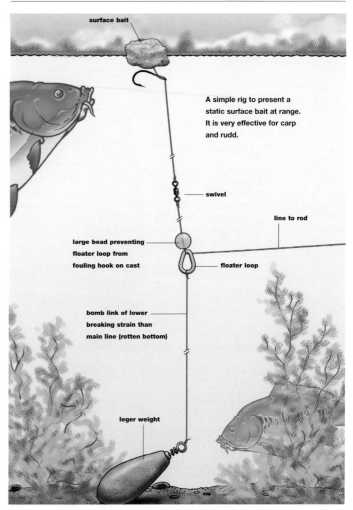

surface bait

A simple rig to present a static surface bait at range. It is very effective for carp and rudd.

swivel

line to rod

large bead preventing floater loop from fouling hook on cast

floater loop

bomb link of lower breaking strain than main line (rotten bottom)

leger weight

ABOVE: The principle of the anchored floating bait is simple in concept but it can be quite difficult to use in practice. It is really only needed when fish are moving on the surface, but there is a strong wind that blows the bait away from them. The best baits are chunks of bread crust or high-protein floaters that rise easily.

obviously a snagged line waiting to happen. It is always best, therefore, for the last 2 ft (60 cm) of the lead link to be of very weak mono, about 3 lb (1.36 kg), so that the lead breaks away easily if it does become hung up when you are playing a fish. If you do try this technique, do not use your best leads.

A variety of leads

Fly Fishing

At one time or another, most coarse fish can be taken fly fishing. The species most susceptible to this approach in rivers are chub, rudd, dace and grayling, and all these can be taken on either dry or wet fly depending on the day and the insects that are hatching. Chub are very appreciative of large patterns offering a substantial mouthful, and mayfly imitations in season, as well as large white moth and sedge patterns at dusk. They are also suckers for Pheasant Tail nymphs. Roach and dace will take any small dry fly pattern over streamy shallows. Grayling are very receptive to the dry fly, or standard wet fly such as Mallard and Claret, and also nymphs such as the Montana or Pheasant Tail.

Most fly-caught coarse fish will obviously be accidental captures taken when fishing trout reservoirs, but some of these are eye openers. Fly fishing with lures has proved one of the deadliest methods of taking perch. The most famous lure of all time for perch fishing was developed by the famous fisherman Richard Walker at Hanningfield Reservoir in Essex, called, not surprisingly, the Hanningfield lure. It was designed to imitate fry with two hooks in tandem, and is fished fairly deep in the water. Since then, most of the big trout waters have produced large perch that have fallen to lures fished on fast-sinking lines, three of the best patterns being Jack Frost, Sweeney Todd and Polystickle.

Lures and nymphs have also taken their share of roach and bream from trout reservoirs, while more and more anglers are targeting pike on large lures, drawn across reed beds, presumably to imitate the flapping of young ducklings. Fishing for pike like this obviously requires a wire trace, and it is better to use a trace of around 30 lb (13.6 kg). Lighter traces can be used but they are prone to kinking because of the continual casting required.

On intimate stillwaters, carp and rudd, when present, are frequently caught by anglers fly fishing – especially rudd, which are more tolerant of the heavy fly line than many other species.

TOP: A north country river that holds good chub, dace and grayling. Wet fly is the favoured form of presentation and the angler here is casting across under the trees.

ABOVE: Many good perch are caught in trout reservoirs, usually on lures fished deep which they take for fry. Perch are a fine sporting fish and this is a good specimen.

Legering

Although basic freelining is an effective technique in ideal circumstances, it has inherent weaknesses. The casting range is obviously limited and will be dictated by the size of bait. Even with a large bait it will never be more than a modest distance, with the exception of freelined deadbaits for pike or catfish. Secondly, with a slack line out, it is sometimes impossible to tighten properly to the bait, and bite detection can be very hit and miss. This can lead to the unsatisfactory situation of the bait being moved a short distance before any indication is seen at the rod. This is unsafe as it has the potential for deep hooking. Bite-offs, when the fish sever the hooklink with their throat teeth can occur all too easily and all anglers know how easily perch, for instance, gorge baits.

ABOVE: Waiting for a bite. The contemplative angler sits beside the river as the water flows gently past him. Could any day be spent in more pleasant surroundings?

Using Leads

These problems are largely minimized by legering, which simply means using lead on the terminal tackle. This increases casting range and makes early bite indication more likely as the lead allows the slack in the line to be tightened up.

In its simplest forms, legering can be subdivided into fixed or running leads. A simple fixed-lead leger could be pinching two swan shot on the line 4 in (10 cm) from the hook – still an effective presentation for winter chub – while the simplest running leger could be using a standard Arlesey bomb leger weight, with the line free to run through the swivel. This is stopped by a bead above the swivel of the hooklink. This simple running

lead overcomes the problems of missed bites at range, the principle being that, as line is taken by a fish, it pulls through the swivel of the lead, giving early bite warning in whichever direction the fish is moving. The heavier the lead you use the more this will be true, because of its increased inertia.

There are many permutations and refinements of these basic legering principles to meet differing water conditions, such as heavy bottom weed. Each one is designed to allow easily adjusted bait presentation and to encourage timidly biting fish to give good bite indications. In the following pages are basic legering techniques that cover 99 per cent of the angling situations you are likely to encounter.

Sliding Link

The sliding-link leger is a natural progression from the running bomb, and entails the weight being mounted on a separate link rather than on the main line itself. The simplest link leger of all is to pinch swan shot on to a doubled length of nylon, leaving a small loop in the nylon through which the main line runs. This is stopped from sliding to the hook by either a leger stop or a small shot.

The advantages of this arrangement over the lead being on the main line are twofold. Firstly, if you wish to change the amount of lead, there is no need to break down the terminal rig, you simply add or subtract the amount of shot. Secondly, in the event of snagging, the shots

Making a Simple Sliding Link

1 To make a simple sliding link you just need split shot, nylon monofilament and a hook.

2 Cut off a short length of nylon, fold it in half and pinch on the shot as shown, leaving a small loop.

3 Slide the link on to the main line and tie on the hook. Place a stop shot on the main line where required.

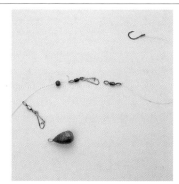

1 You will need snap-link swivels, a suitable leger weight, nylon, hook and a rubber bead.

2 Tie the hooklink to the swivel. Place snap-link swivel and bead up the main line; tie in the second swivel.

3 Attach the hooklink to the bottom snap link. Clip the leger weight to the sliding snap link.

will pull off the nylon link, very often allowing recovery of the hook.

When you need to use lead more substantial than a few shot, the nylon loop is substituted for a snap-link swivel on the main line, which allows different leger weights to be clipped and unclipped in seconds. The extra mass means that it is rarely satisfactory to stop them above the hook by simple leger stops or split shot as they continually slip.

It is far better to prepare separate hooklinks with their own swivels, with a rubber shock bead between the swivel and the sliding lead link to protect the knots. For even greater versatility, terminate the main line with a second swivel and snap link, to which the hooklink swivel attaches. With this arrangement, not only can you change leads in seconds, but you can also change hooklinks as quickly.

Another variation on this principle is to attach the lead to a short length of nylon and a swivel before attaching it to the main line snap link. This is always used with the nylon link of low breaking strain, known as a "rotten bottom", the idea being that if the lead becomes trapped in a snag it will break away but leave the main terminal rig in place. Use this arrangement if adding a lead link for freelining for pike.

A further extension is to make the nylon link much longer – up to several feet – if you are trying to cope with deep bottom weed or silt in a still water, and combine that with a hookbait of neutral buoyancy so that it comes to rest gently on the weed or

silt, while the lead link sinks through it to the lake bottom, anchoring the rig in place. Again, this would usually incorporate a link of lower breaking strain than the main line. If you want to get really fancy, you can also place a balsa float body free-running on the lead link, ensuring that the main line is kept up in the water away from the bottom debris.

Fixed Paternoster

What differentiates the paternoster from link legers is that, whereas link legers have the lead on the main line above the hook, the paternoster is the opposite. They are weight-forward arrangements, with the hooklink above the lead. An example from modern carp fishing is the helicopter rig, designed for ultra-long casting with heavy leads. In this case, the distance from hooklink swivel to lead is usually shorter than the hooklink, but as it is a weight-forward arrangement it can be classed as belonging to the paternoster family.

When you have the problem of deep bottom weed or silt, the paternoster is a better solution, and far easier to cast than the sliding link. This will be incorporated with a free-running or semi-fixed hooklink several feet above the lead link, which again will be of lighter line than the main line in order to give the "rotten bottom" effect if necessary.

A semi-fixed hooklink can be created by connecting it to a run bead and plugging that to the lead swivel with silicon tubing, or by tying a stop knot and bead above the hooklink,

effectively jamming it. A fish pulling hard enough can move the hooklink in both cases, hence the "semi-fixed" label. Semi-fixed links often give more positive bite indication.

As the paternoster is a more aerodynamic rig than the standard link arrangement, it is the one to choose when long casting is required, and as long-range fishing often carries with it extra difficulty in seeing and hooking bites efficiently, the rig usually incorporates fairly short fixed hooklinks of only a few inches, which encourage positive bites. The fixed short hooklink paternoster has become a standard approach for still-water bream and tench anglers. This would normally include a heavy lead of at least 2 oz (50 g), pulling the line as tight as possible and using a heavy butt indicator. For stillwater bream especially, hooking on this arrangement is 100 per cent successful, most bites being sudden drops back of the indicator as a fish lifting the bait relaxes the tension in the tackle. The fixed hooklink would normally be tied into the main line using water knots.

Bolt Rig

Where educated or nervous fish are giving tentative bites on normal legering tactics, often referred to as "twitch" bites, you have to find a way of accentuating the bites you are getting by encouraging the fish to move off with the bait in a more positive manner. The short hooklink paternoster encourages positive bites when used with a heavy lead and in

Making a Fixed Paternoster Rig

1 To make a fixed paternoster you will just require a leger weight or feeder, nylon monofilament and hook.

2 Tie the hooklink the required distance from the main line, using a water knot.

3 Attach the leger weight, or feeder if you are using one, to the end of the main line.

4 Feeders can be used in a paternoster instead of a leger.

5 The completed rig, as step 3, with a feeder instead of a weight.

fact this could be considered to be a type of bolt rig, as indeed can the carp angler's helicopter rig. The name originated because the purpose of the rigs is to make the fish bolt with the baits in their mouths, thereby giving unmistakable indications.

Pure bolt rigs, however, take that general principle one stage further in that they will normally feature the bait mounted on a hair rig with the hook itself being bare, so that the hook point pricking the fish further encourages it to bolt.

The standard bolt rig is very similar to the earliest leger arrangement of a running or semi-fixed lead on the main line above the hooklink, although the bolt features a much heavier lead than is actually needed for the cast, coupled with a very short hooklink of about 6 in (15 cm). It is fair to say that such rigs are mainly used by carp anglers, although they are becoming more in

vogue with barbel anglers fishing statically for bigger-than-average fish.

One adaptation, which is now the most often used rig by carp anglers, is to swap the normal bomb leger weight for an in-line, drilled streamlined lead, which is very resistant to snagging. These leads are used with stiff tubing through the centre, through which the main line passes, this tubing being connected by silicon tubing to the hooklink swivel to make the lead semi-fixed.

Most anglers using bolt rigs will do so in combination with braided or dacron hooklinks, and if long casting is involved, a substantial problem exists as the limp hooklink materials will tangle around the main line. To overcome this, these rigs usually incorporate a length of rig tubing longer than the hooklink above the lead. During flight, the heavy lead obviously flies in advance, with the hooklink trailing behind. It is at this

stage that the anti-tangle tube prevents the link curling around the main line. If you want to avoid tubing but still use braids, another solution is to use a setting gel that quickly dissolves in water. Some gels stiffen the link for casting, but revert to normal after a few minutes' immersion in the water.

Feeder Bolt Rig

There are three variations of the feeder bolt rig for use in stillwaters, the most commonly used being, in essence, identical to the short hooklink paternoster, with a heavy swimfeeder replacing the lead. This is the rig that has become a standard for stillwater roach anglers, and has solved the problem of missed bites. It normally features a light hooklink about 18 in (45 cm) above a 2 oz (50 g) blockend feeder, baited with maggots or casters. After casting, the line is drawn tight, a heavy butt indicator attached, and most bites are indicated by a dramatic drop back.

The second version has an in-line swimfeeder on the main line 18 in (45 cm) above the hooklink, with a 2 oz (50 g) bomb on the end of the line, as in a normal paternoster. When the cast has been made, the action of drawing the tackle tight invariably pulls the terminal rig a little way towards the bank. In the first arrangement, this will pull the hookbait away from the maggots escaping from the swimfeeder whereas in this case, it pulls the hook towards the free offerings. This is a small point that could make all the difference on a hard day.

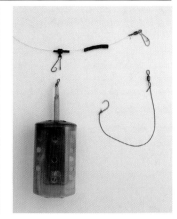

1 The components required are hook-link material, leger weight or feeder, swivels, snap links, silicon tubing, a bolt bead snap link and a hook.

2 Tie the hooklink to the hook and swivel. Slide the bolt-bead snap link up the main line, then the silicon tubing. Attach second snap-link swivel.

3 Make sure that the hooklink is the correct length and then attach the leger weight or swimfeeder to the top link.

4 The completed bolt rig using a swimfeeder.

5 The completed bolt rig using a leger weight.

6 The completed bolt rig with a lead and a hair loop at the hook.

When roach fishing in either of these styles, which could see only 2 lb (0.91 kg) hooklinks and size 16 hooks, it is fatal to strike as such, as it is easy to crack off on a tight line. It is sufficient to simply lift the rod and start playing the fish. It is also one of those occasions to backwind rather than use a clutch.

Casting heavy feeders requires a main line of at least 6 lb (2.72 kg) breaking strain, and it is impossible to set a clutch to suit a 2 lb (0.91 kg) hooklink in these circumstances. To protect the light hooklinks during the playing of a big roach, or anything else that takes the bait for that matter, many anglers insert a short length of

power gum or pole elastic above the hooklink as a shock absorber.

The third bolt-feeder arrangement is very much in vogue these days, especially on commercial small carp fisheries, and it is called the method feeder rig. A ball of groundbait and mixed feed particles is moulded round a special method feeder and the hookbait, invariably mounted on a very short hooklink, is pushed into the side of the feed. The idea is that the fish start rooting around in the bait, breaking it down, and the hookbait is taken quite naturally as it falls free of the whole. It is a devastating presentation and has led to many large catches.

7 The bolt rig ready to fish with a boilie mounted on the hair rig.

The Knotless Knot

The knotless knot or 'no knot' is widely used by carp and specimen hunters when presenting baits like boilies on a hair rig. It is so called because no knot is actually tied and the whole tying relies on tension and whipping to keep it in place. It allows the angler to incorporate the use of a hair rig on to the hook without the need to tie off a separate knot for the hook, and then a separate knot for the hair. The knotless knot provides both in the same tying sequence. To make the best of this knot it is advised that the hair loop is tied into a length of hooklength material and that the bait is actually mounted on to the hair, before the hook is tied in, as shown in this sequence. Doing this allows the angler to measure out an exact distance for the hair in relation to the size of the bait and the hook used.

Once the bait has been mounted on to the hair, the free end of the hooklength is passed through the eye of the hook and the baited hair is lined up with the back of the shank on the hook. When it is in the correct position the 'no knot' can be tied. With the bait in the correct position the angler would be well advised to whip the hooklength line around the hook shank, trapping the hair, in a manner that takes the hooklength line away from any join in the eye of the hook. This stops the hooklength line biting into a groove and doing any damage to the hooklength material.

Once the line has been whipped around the shank six to eight times the end of the hooklength is passed back down through the eye of the hook. When pulled tight, the tension holds in place both the hook and the hair rig. For added security a dab of strong glue can be used on the finished whipping. It is important that the hooklength is passed back through the eye in a downward fashion. Doing this ensures that the hook is held at an offset angle, and this allows a better hooking presentation. This knot can only be used with eyed hooks, as it is the eye of the hook that provides the anchorage hold for the hooklength.

ABOVE: You will need: scissors, hooklink material, boilie stops, boilie needle, swivel and a hook.

Presenting a Pop-up Boilie with a Knotless Knot

1 A completed knotless knot tied with a pop-up boilie. This knot is easy to tie, and reliable.

2 Here a small silicon sleeve has been threaded on to the hooklink and over the shoulder of the hook.

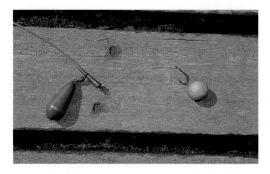

3 The sleeve holds the hair rig in place. The hair rig is attached to the lead and the rig is now ready to cast.

4 The cast has been made and the boilie rises "popped-up" from the bottom.

Tying the Knotless Knot

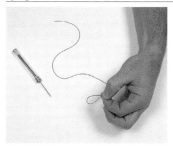

1 Form a loop in the end of the hooklink. Hold it in place between thumb and forefinger.

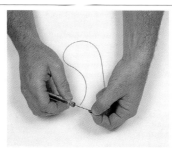

2 Pass this loop around the line to form a second loop. Pull first loop through and catch it with the needle.

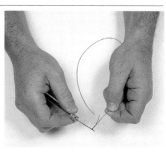

3 Pull the first loop tight making a tight loop in the hooklink and trim off the spare end.

4 Select the boilie that you want to use and then push the boilie on to the needle.

5 Pass the boilie needle through hooklink loop so that the boilie can be threaded on to the hooklink.

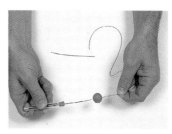

6 Pull the boilie over the loop so that it lies on the hooklink, ready for the next stage.

7 Push the boilie stop through the loop, and pull it tight to hold the boilie securely in place.

8 Thread the hooklink through the eye of the hook and position it the required distance from the boilie.

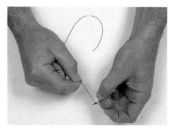

9 Tightly whip seven turns of line around the hook shank and hair rig. Ensure the turns are even.

10 Pass the end of the hooklink back through the hook eye.

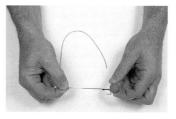

11 Pull tight and the knotless knot is now complete.

12 Attach swivel to the hooklink and the rig is now ready.

Touch Legering

Although the quivertip is certainly the most common form of bite detection when legering in flowing water, there is no method of bite detection that can match the sensitivity of touch legering, especially at night.

Touch legering requires some current to tension the line and requires practice to perfect, but once mastered you will find that no other method of bite detection gives such an instant warning. This applies equally upstream or down. For normal downstreaming, the urgent tightening of the line acts like an electric shock, while in the upstreaming situation, the sudden removal of tension from line that was as taut as a banjo string is equally unmistakable.

Initially, take a few trips to an easy river, one perhaps containing a good head of medium-sized chub. With bites plentiful, you will soon experience the range of bite variations. It is a good idea to touch leger without a quivertip in daylight to start with, as it is a good grounding for when you start fishing after dark and your fingers provide the only early-warning system.

There are two methods of touch legering, both equally efficient. The one you choose depends on personal preference. You can crook a little line

Ways of Touch Legering

1 Touch legering with the line held on the forefinger of the right hand holding the rod.

2 Touch legering with the line held in the left hand. The choice of method is entirely personal.

over the index finger of the hand holding the rod or you may prefer to take a loop of line in the other hand.

Bites on your fingers are generally unmistakable, an initial pluck being followed by a slow draw. Occasionally, however, you will experience a succession of small plucks and often these will be so delicate that no indication is seen on the rod top. These are sometimes caused by fish rolling the bait in the mouth and a strike can provide a bonus fish. More often, however, small bites take the form of fast jabs, particularly from suspicious fish in hard-fished stretches. There is a high percentage of missed bites when striking at these

indications. In these circumstances, a switch to upstreaming often works, as you are then waiting for the collapse of the line tension over your fingers, which is easier to detect.

For the most efficient touch legering, arrange for the rod top to be pointing at the bait as much as possible, although modern frictionless rod rings make this less vital than it used to be. The shallower the line angle, the more direct contact you have with your quarry. Touch legering, especially in the dark, is fascinating fishing.

BELOW: Fishing the swimfeeder at long range on a stillwater.

Swimfeeder Fishing

Although the feeder has wide application in stillwaters, the orthodox application of the swimfeeder is in streamy water, where its use is in ensuring a constant flow of bait down the current. A general rig arrangement is exactly the same as a sliding link with snap link swivels, the swimfeeder merely replacing the lead. In summer, feeder fishing in fast-running water is more effective the more often you cast and the more bait you use. This is particularly true when using maggots and the minimum bait to use is 4 pints (2.28 litres). Cost is obviously a limiting factor, but this is one technique where you can buy your bait.

Streamer Beds

Streamer beds are particularly good feeder swims, as careful positioning of each cast between streamer tresses ensures that the loose feed continually follows the same narrow band. Accuracy of casting with a feeder, and then ensuring it remains put after settling, gives the most efficient presentation possible. To prevent rolling, oval blockends are good for streamer work, and you may also want to carry a selection of clip-on leads to cope with brisker than normal flows. Use as long a tail as possible, up to 3 ft (90 cm), so that the maggot hookbait is free to follow the same undulating path as the streamer tresses. The density of the vegetation will be the limiting factor for how long that link can be before it becomes a handicap. Always fish the feeder free-running. Fixed blockends do not travel easily through streamer roots.

Main Species

The species of interest to the summer river feeder angler are roach, dace, bream, chub and barbel, and for all those species, except barbel, ready-tied super spades, in sizes 12 to 16, to 4.5 lb (2 kg) nylon are recommended. For barbel, a size 12 super spade is appropriate, but tie it to a minimum of 6 lb (2.72 kg) invisible line.

As well as maggots, feeder techniques are effective with all other baits, using open-ended feeders loaded with suitable loose feed. Obviously, open-ended work is best utilized in the streamier flows, where the current does the important bait distribution work. Of the larger baits, bread flake fished on a longish tail, in conjunction with a mixture of liquidized bread, grilled hemp and milk powder for visual attraction is a favourite. If you are using a flavoured bait, make sure that the feed is similarly flavoured.

Open-ended feeder work with particles is carried out in conjunction with "exploding" groundbait plugs, which blow the particles free of the feeder. This is achieved by the simple expedient of mixing the normal liquidized bread/additive combination with a quantity of dry sausage rusk. Only moments after the cast, the rusk absorbs water so quickly that it rapidly expands, causing an underwater bait explosion. The most used particles with the open-ended feeder are casters and sweetcorn.

Winter Fishing

Feeder applications for winter fishing will follow similar lines when water temperatures are good, although maggots are used far more in the winter than in summer, when other particles are favoured, as small fish are far less troublesome.

The obvious differences in winter are sparser weed growth, enhanced height and flow speeds, and lower water temperatures, factors which affect winter feed rates. Approach depends entirely on water temperature. If favourable, even more bait than normal is used, to offset the dispersal effect of the flow. For winter chub or barbel fishing, a gallon of maggots would not be too much when recasting every few minutes throughout the day. The other important detail is to ensure that your feeder consistently presents the stream of bait down the same line. The faster the current, the easier it is to get this vital ingredient of successful feeder fishing wrong. Do not be afraid to pile lead on the feeder to ensure that it stays put. Bait that is scattered all over the river because the feeder is too light, and rolling all over the place, is worse than useless. This is when flat-bottomed feeders come into their own.

Another feature of winter fishing with the feeder, when the weed is much sparser, is that you can use lighter hooklinks, and this can make all the difference in clear water.

When the water temperature is 40°F (5°C) or less, and the water is low and clear, maggots fished in conjunction with the feeder can be one of the most effective methods for chub, roach, dace and grayling, but the clarity of water demands the finest terminal rig you can safely use. A size 16 Super Spade to 18 in (45 cm) of 2.6 lb (1.18 kg) mono is typical.

The quantity of free feed should be cut right back, and you should use a far smaller feeder in winter so that there really is the most modest trickle of loose maggots becoming available at any one time. In very cold water, though, even the maggots become lethargic, and it pays to enlarge the holes in the feeder to facilitate the ease with which they can escape.

Making a Sliding Swimfeeder

1 You need: snap-link swivels, rubber bead, swimfeeder, nylon, a hook. First tie hooklink to swivel, then place the feeder up the main line.

2 Add the bead, then tie in the snap-link swivel to the end of the main line. Finally attach the hooklink to the bottom snap link.

Upstream Legering

It is true to say that 99 per cent of all legering on rivers is carried out downstream, with bites being signalled by the quivertip pulling round. Much of the time, however, an upstream presentation is superior, for example when dealing with jabs on the rod top which prove difficult or impossible to hit, the kind of indication common with roach at short range. The upstream presentation will see all resistance removed when the fish pulls the bait downstream, so it holds on to the bait for that vital few moments longer.

A second major advantage of upstream legering is that it can automatically locate a hot spot in a swim, by periodically shifting the lead so that it bumps down the flow. Natural obstructions such as rises in the gravel bed and weed roots will halt the progress of the lead.

When legering downstream, most anglers sit upstream of the swim and fish each area in turn by casting across and down to it, and this simple method catches fish consistently. However, there are weaknesses associated with a succession of down and across presentations. First, as you cast to each area in turn, there is the initially alarming effect of a lead plummeting into the swim. Obviously, the fish soon recover their composure if they are feeding hard, but it is nevertheless a frightening effect you can do without. You may decide to cut down the amount of casting by rolling the bait into position rather than casting directly to the swim. You can do this by casting to the far bank, fishing that side for a while and then, by lifting the rod point, encourage the terminal rig to roll across river to search other areas. Although this minimizes disturbance, the tautness in the tackle means that, when the bait rolls into midstream and then into the near bank, it does so in an arc across the flow. This is highly unnatural and could be enough to dissuade a suspicious fish from intercepting the bait. Also, the bait will only ever fish on the line of each arc, and in a big swim this can mean a lot of water being unfished.

Upstreaming largely overcomes these objections. Sit at the furthest downstream extremity of the swim and cast two yards above the upstream point of the swim on the far bank. After the lead has settled, the intention is to work the bait progressively down the flow, allowing it to settle for perhaps five minutes and then repeating this at intervals down the run or where a natural feature halts the lead's progress. To do this, the rod point is lifted, and a little line is drawn which dislodges the lead so that it bumps downstream into the required position. That is the first difference to note. The lead bumps downstream in a straight line rather than moving in an arc because the upstream presentation has allowed the creation of slack line when the lead is disturbed.

The entire far bank run could be searched in this progressive manner, every inch of bottom having been covered perfectly naturally and without once having to cast directly at a feeding fish. The next move is to cover the midstream run and near bank run in the same way.

Using Different Leads

For efficient upstream legering, the standard snap-link leger gives the ability to change leads quickly. This is important as a single swim may require a different lead at different points along its length to attain the correct presentation. The lead must be such that it holds steadily against the flow, but only requires a gentle

BELOW: **A barbel swim on the River Thames, best fished upstream.**

pull to be dislodged. Once disturbed, it should quickly settle again and not wash downstream too easily. Generally speaking, if the lead moves a couple of feet downstream and then re-settles, you have it about right.

The quivertip is essential for efficient upstreaming. Work on the principle that you need a 4 in (10 cm) upstream deflection in the tip to be maintainable before the lead yields to the pressure and bumps downstream.

Bites are normally a bump on the tip followed by a kickback due to relaxation of tension.

Certain static situations demand the upstream leger. These include slacks behind rush beds or rafts, or fishing the downstream areas of a line of bushes or trees. Often, the only efficient approach is from downstream of the swim. Reliable winter swims are a "V" of quiet water created by mid-river rush beds.

ABOVE: A lively weir pool much loved by both fish and fishermen. This type of water is ideal for presenting a bait on an upstream leger – use a weight of lead that holds against the flow, but is easily dislodged by a pull.

This area can be tiny, so aim for the bait to fish at the point of the "V" in normal flow, or tighter behind the obstruction at higher levels.

You do not want the bait to move once it is in position, and it pays to use a little more lead in these places when fishing a steady glide. The reason is that although the bait is fishing an area of quieter water, often an intervening faster flow has to be taken into account.

Upstreaming is vulnerable to false bites if there is much flotsam in the river. It takes very little drifting weed to dislodge a critically balanced terminal rig. If this is a problem, and it is quite likely to be so in a flood, put more lead on than normal, and try to ignore the rubbish hitting the line. A bite from a big fish will still be obvious. These conditions are ideal for barbel, and you won't mistake bites from those.

LEFT: Using an upstream leger in winter, searching out chub behind a weed raft.

Pole Fishing

A pole is simply a rod without a reel, with the line attached directly to the end of the pole and spare sections added to the butt section to present a bait delicately or to give extra cushioning effect to any bigger fish you might hook. Long poles are available so you can easily fish the far bank of a fairly wide river. When a fish is hooked, if it requires netting, it is brought close enough by dismantling the butt of the pole section by section.

When to Use a Pole

Despite the fact that quite big fish can be landed on the pole, it is essentially a technique best suited for small- to medium-sized fish and is not suitable for specimen hunting. Match fishing, where speed fishing for small fish is vitally important, is where the pole comes into its own.

Its advantage is in the accuracy and delicacy of bait presentation it allows. It is possible, for example, to place a bait right under the foliage of the far bank of a canal. As there is very little line in the water between float and pole top, problems with wind or drift are largely eliminated, allowing you to keep your bait tight to your loose feed at all times. Tackle can be very fine indeed, and because of the close control, floats need only have whisker-fine tips, shotted down so that the merest flicker from a small fish is registered.

There are three types of pole assembly: put in, put over and telescopic. The first two are relevant to long poles, the put-over joints being the better arrangement. In this, the smaller end near the tip fits over the thinner section of the next section down and so on. This arrangement gives a uniform taper. The put over has two advantages. First, if the joint starts to wear, the thinner section, being on the lower joint, merely inserts slightly deeper and is still a good fit.

In the "put in" arrangement, the top sections fit in to the lower sections and not over. Joint wear could see the entire thinner section sliding into the one below it, making an expensive pole unusable. The other disadvantage of "put in" is that, like a normal rod spigot, the thinner section has a parallel taper on the joint section for a snug fit, but this makes unshipping butt sections very difficult when the pole is flexed with a bigger-than-average fish.

Telescopic poles are much shorter, to a maximum of around 23 ft (7m) and are known as whips.

Poles and Whips

There are a tremendous number of poles available and as with all things in life, you get what you pay for.

Poles

Pay as much as you can afford. As cheaper poles can be either too heavy, too fragile or too floppy, they can be difficult and inefficient to use. As a general principle, the lighter and stiffer the pole is, the more relaxing it will be. Always give consideration to the type of fishing you will be doing, before buying. A match angler might opt for a very stiff and light pole, which he can hold effortlessly for the duration of the contest, whereas the pleasure angler targeting carp needs a little more flexibility in the tip. The latter would be the choice for the all rounder, but the pole must come with a "spare top three" kit.

This means that you have the option of using the spare three top joints fitted with stronger elastic (see pages 101–3). In a situation where you are fishing with, say, a number 3 elastic for small bream and decent tench move into the swim, you might need a heavier grade elastic, say number 8. Rather than breaking down the rig, it is far quicker and easier to replace it with spare top sections, which are already rigged with the heavier grade. The top match anglers will carry several spare "top threes"

rigged with different elastics, in order to save valuable fishing time.

The elastic used in pole fishing is the shock absorber, as you cannot give line as you can with rod and reel. With fine elastics 1 and 2 for small fish, you need only rig the tip section. Elastics 3 to 6 are preferably set inside the top two sections, while the top three sections should be rigged with the heavier elastic grades when bigger fish are expected.

Whips

With telescopic whips, it is impossible to remove sections once you are fishing. The bottom sections can only be removed by sliding them over the top, and you therefore set the length before fishing commences. You could, for instance, fish a 13 ft (4 m) whip using the top four sections of a 23 ft (7 m) assembly. Match anglers would again carry several different length whips. Elastics are not used because top sections, known as "flick tips", are ultra fine. The line is fitted directly to the flick tip by first passing it through two lengths of fine silicon tubing. The first length is slid over the tip, trapping the end of the line, which is then wound round the tip several times before the second length of tubing is slid halfway over the end.

Tackle

Pole fishing requires a good deal of specialist tackle.

Bungs, Bushes and Connectors

Elastic is anchored at the base of the appropriate pole section with a bung. In the case of the "put over" pole, the bung must be sited far enough inside the pole section so that it does not interfere with the fitting of the next section. It is fitted with a strong length of nylon for removing it. At the pole tip, the elastic runs through a PTFE (Teflon) bush, which must fit the tip snugly. As tips are usually uncut, trim it a fraction at a time until the bush will barely fit the hole. It should have the smallest practical bore for the elastic. Finish with fine wet-and-dry sandpaper. Where the elastic emerges from the pole tip, it must be secured in a Stonflo tip connector, a little device attaching the elastic to the terminal rig nylon.

Elastics

Elastics come in ten grades, numbered 1–6, plus 8, 10, 12 and 14, ranging from 2.5 lb (1.13 kg) breaking strain to 16 lb (7.26 kg) for number 14. It is very important to keep pole bushes as clean as possible, and apply a little pole-elastic lubricant before each fishing session.

Pole Floats

In general terms, pole float design follows the rules for ordinary floats. For stillwaters you would generally opt for a body-down design with a longish tip for stability; for canals with a little drift, or very slow rivers, the classic shallow oval or stick float is appropriate; while for faster-flowing rivers you need the body-up design of the Avon float. Obviously, pole floats are far smaller, and extensive ranges are available. Most pole anglers have their various rigs, plus spares, made up on winders for quick changing.

Although the top match anglers will use pole floats with very fine wire or bristle tips for ultimate sensitivity, they are extremely difficult to shot correctly, and the pleasure angler is better off selecting a float with a more substantial tip. Also, pole stem material can be important. For fishing hard on the bottom, a wire-stemmed float gives more stability, whereas a carbon-stemmed design gives a slower terminal rig descent for fishing "on the drop".

Most anglers use three lengths of silicon tubing to secure the float to the main line to prevent float slippage when playing a fish. The bottom piece normally overlaps the float base to eliminate tangles.

Pole Weights

These will be either small split shot, styl weights or olivettes. Styls are sausage-shaped and need to be put on the rig with special pliers. Olivettes are pear-shaped with a centre bore and are usually used as bulk shot with tiny split shot at the business end. They are available non-bored with bristle ends, so that they can be fitted to the line with two bits of fine silicon tubing for quick weight adjustment.

Pole Hooks

Hook sizes rarely exceed size 16 for pole fishing, although anglers who are pole fishing carp fisheries with pastes may go as big as size 8. In the smaller sizes, from 16–22 eyed hooks are too bulky and a more delicate presentation is achieved with spade-end patterns. For casters, maggots and hemp, the normal choice is sizes 18–22 fine wire hooks, with hemp mounted on a wide-gape pattern. Bread and paste baits would normally be fished using a longer shank hook with an in-curved point.

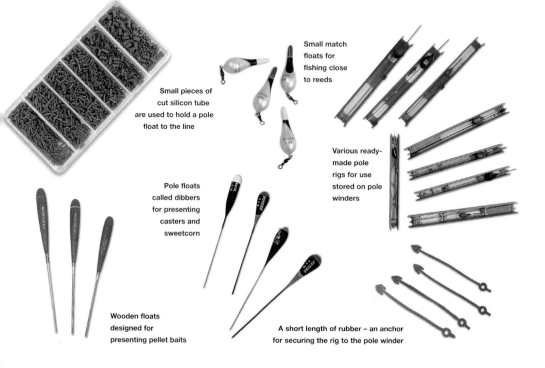

Small pieces of cut silicon tube are used to hold a pole float to the line

Small match floats for fishing close to reeds

Various ready-made pole rigs for use stored on pole winders

Pole floats called dibbers for presenting casters and sweetcorn

Wooden floats designed for presenting pellet baits

A short length of rubber – an anchor for securing the rig to the pole winder

Lines

Main lines and hook lengths should be balanced to the pole elastic when they are in use. For instance, if you were using a very fine number 2 elastic, you would want no thicker than 0.08 mm Pro Micron, whereas you could double that diameter if fishing a size 14 elastic.

Pole Rollers

When fishing the longer poles, you will need a roller behind you to take the weight. The technique with a roller is to first find the balance point of the pole when sitting on your box. Then place the roller at the end of the pole. This means that, when pushing the pole backwards, the weight is supported at all times and, when pulling it forwards to put a bait out the pole will be balanced when it comes off the roller, which avoids jerking as you take the weight.

Pole Cups

For accurate loose feeding, a clip-on pole cup is invaluable. Place the selected feed in the cup, clip it to the pole, and deposit it at exactly the right place. Nothing could be simpler.

Catapults

For constant drip feeding of bait samples, a fine latex catapult is invaluable. A catapult with a mini or micro pouch is perfect for delivering a few maggots or casters at one time.

Pole Elastic

When playing a fish while using a pole all the shock of the fish fighting the hook is absorbed through an internal elastic. The type used will depend on the size of the species the pole angler is fishing for. Small, silver fish, such as roach and small bream, "skimmers", need a size 3 or 4 elastic. When it comes to tench or carp, a heavy elastic with a rating of 8, 10 or even 12 would be the right choice.

To elasticate the pole you will need the following equipment: the elastic of the number you require; a bung to go at the base of the pole section; a PTFE (hard plastic) bush to fit the tip of the pole; a connector to join the elastic to the end tackle; a fine wire elastic threader used to thread the elastic through the pole

How to Elasticate a Pole

1 Here a number eight elastic has been selected as the pole is to be elasticated for small carp. Alongside the elastic are a bung, bung retractor, PTFE tip and a connector.

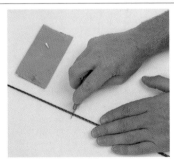

2 As the pole is to be fitted with a heavy-grade elastic, the tip should be cut back to accommodate this. If the tip were left at its full length, there is a possibility that it might snap if a bigger carp were hooked.

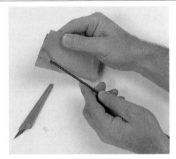

3 Score the outer wall of the pole tip. Once the whole circumference of the pole tip has been scored, it can be snapped. The cut-back tip section should then be cleaned with a small piece of fine sandpaper.

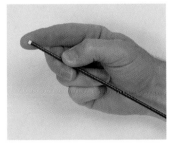

4 The PTFE bush tip is then inserted into the end of the tip. You may find trial and error is the only way you are going to get an exact fit. If this is the case, cut away a small bit of the tip section at a time, until you arrive at the right fit for the PTFE tip.

5 Thread the wire elastic threader through the tip section and out at the base of the second or third section of the pole. The end of the threader has a diamond eye. This will grip the elastic while it is being drawn up through the inside of the pole.

6 Once the elastic has been drawn through the inner walls of the pole sections, the bung can be fitted. A simple overhand knot should be used to form a loop, which can be fitted to the bung.

sections; a modelling knife, and wet-and-dry sandpaper that is used to clean off any rough edges. A special bung retractor can also be used with certain bungs so that they can be removed easily at a later stage.

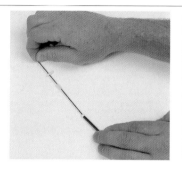

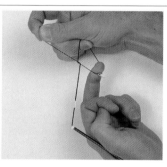

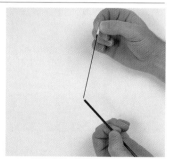

7 Some bungs come complete with a bung remover. As this pole is of a put-over type, the bung is inserted up inside the wall of the pole. At some stage the bung will have to be retrieved to change the elastic.

8 Take the end of the elastic at the tip end, draw it taut until a small amount of tension is placed on it. For this size of elastic, the connector needs to be fitted so that the elastic is just placed under tension.

9 Thread on the connector sleeve and then the elastic through the hole in the connector. Secure the elastic to the connector using a granny knot. Make sure the knot does not slip.

10 With the knot secured, slide the sleeve down over the connector to protect the knot. Now test the elastic for a smooth, bump-free exit from the pole tip.

11 To join a pole rig to the connector, simply slide back the sleeve and fit the loop at the top end of the rig on to the hook. Once in place, close the sleeve to trap the line.

ABOVE: Olivettes are very good for fishing in deep water or to get the bait to the bottom very quickly. There are several different sizes of olivette available to the pole angler. The choice of weight will be governed by the depth of water and the size of the pole float being used.

Holding a Pole and Landing a Fish

1 The pole being used is 44 ft/13.5 m long. The pole is supported in both hands with the left hand under the butt. The angler's back is straight, and the right leg is used as a support.

2 The back view shows how the right leg serves as a platform for the pole to rest on. The angler's body is slightly turned to the right for comfort. The tip of the pole is just above the water.

3 Contact has been made with a fish, and the angler starts to ship the pole back on to the bank behind. The internal elastic of the pole takes the shock of the fish.

4 Shipping back the pole is done slowly and carefully. The angler must aim to keep the pole moving backwards continuously, maintaining contact with the fish.

5 On the bank behind the angler the butt section of the rod is fed back over a special pole roller. Once the pole reaches the roller, the pole can be pulled in more smoothly.

6 The angler then breaks down the pole by removing the back sections. This is usually at the depth of the rig being used. Small fish can then be swung into the hand and unhooked.

7 LEFT: Larger fish should be netted. Competition anglers always net their fish in case they drop off the hook when they are swung out of the water. Once the fish has been unhooked, the rig can be rebaited and the pole reassembled and shipped back out to the swim.

Stillwater Techniques

You can use either a long pole or a whip on stillwaters. The long pole is best suited to reservoirs and lakes while the whip comes into its own fishing a canal.

Long Pole

Before fishing, make sure you are comfortable with the box at the correct height and the roller positioned correctly. If you are fishing on the bottom, plumb accurately and then mark the line with a marker pen

at the bottom of the float stem. That way, if you come up in the water later, you can re-set the depth easily. Next introduce a little free feed with the pole cup, but do not overdo it at this stage. You can always put more in. but it is impossible to take it out.

When you get your bite, strike firmly upwards to set the hook, remembering that you have to overcome the cushioning effect of the elastic. If it is a small fish, then ship it towards you by removing pole sections until you can swing in or net the fish. However, if a slightly bigger fish pulls elastic from the pole tip, get it under control as soon as possible, pulling it away from the swim to avoid scaring the shoal.

In a situation where you are fishing mid-range with the top few sections of a pole, always keep the butt sections handy, ready to ship out if necessary, if a big fish heads directly away from you. If you get line bites, the fish may have moved up in the water. You can then change to an "on the drop" presentation, with strung out tiny shot. Keep the bait on the move. Once it has settled, bring it to the top and let it drop again.

Whip

Whip fishing in stillwaters is probably most applicable to canals, where 23 ft (7 m) covers most situations. Casting with a whip is normally a case of a simple overhead flick, and landing the fish on these shorter poles is as straightforward as with rod and line. Thirteen feet (4 m) of line at hand means that a small fish can easily be swung to hand for unhooking. It is sometimes difficult to see the advantage of a 13 ft (4 m) whip over a 13 ft (4 m) rod and line, but it must be remembered that a whip is far lighter with an ultra-fine tip, and generally presents an extremely delicate terminal rig.

Even the lightest traditional rod may not have the tip sensitivity to set the hook into quick-biting small fish, or the flexibility to prevent them being bumped off the barbless hooks often used in speed fishing. Also, casting a very light rig with rod and line is far more inaccurate, while the overhead flick cast leads to tangles. Pole cups cannot be used with whips, but regular feeding by hand or a catapult is perfectly accurate at the short ranges involved.

ABOVE: The angler lands a good bream caught on a pole. Note the long terminal rig.

River Techniques

The secrets of successful pole fishing on rivers are the same as for trotting: keeping a steady trickle of feed going in on the right line, ensuring the correct amount and consistency of groundbait, and making sure that the float follows the current without jerking or being pulled off line. In trotting, the overriding principle is to keep contact with the float by having as little line between float and rod top as possible. When "trotting" with the pole you simply follow the float with the pole tip. The restriction is that you cannot fish past the extent of your reach. Another parallel with trotting is that at the end of a trot, a bonus fish often results from holding the float back and making the bait rise in the water. Exactly the same applies to pole work, and by delaying slightly at the end of the run through, as the pole float lifts, the bait will rise, often inducing that bonus bite.

On small to medium rivers, especially those with rush margins, good fish of many species feed tight against the marginal vegetation, and a pole in these circumstances allows presentation that would be impossible with rod and line, no matter how accurate your casting. By consistently running through only inches from the far bank rushes, keeping up a steady feed line at the same time, good catches of fish can be accumulated. Not only is the placement of each bait deadly accurate, it is also disturbance free, two critical factors in efficient angling of any kind. If you are fishing this close to far bank rushes, or even under far bank branches, step up the elastic strength from that which you would normally use. This will give you extra stopping power when the unexpected big chub takes the bait.

Before you start fishing, run your rig through the swim a few times with a bare hook to see if the float buries consistently at one spot, indicating a snag or a rise in the river bed. If you are on a pleasure session, you could move fractionally upstream so that the feature is at the end of the run through. This will mean the float swinging up at the critical point as you hold it back. Also, fish could congregate at the feature as food items become trapped against it. In other words, the bare hook trick could have located a hot spot for you.

With all pole fishing, avoid fishing under power lines. There have already been too many deaths by electrocution. Always take the trouble to warn others.

Groundbait Feeding

Pole fishing is a major part of coarse angling. It is a method used by competition anglers all over the world, and it is also becoming increasingly popular among the ranks of pleasure anglers. It does enable any angler to catch a lot of fish quickly and gives unparalleled control over float and bait placement.

There are many different poles available made in super-light materials up to 53 ft (16 m) in length and their main disadvantage is that they can be difficult to control when there is a strong wind. Correct holding of the pole is vital at all times, when fishing, feeding groundbait, feeding loosefeed or playing a fish. The sequences shown here and on the previous pages show how to do this.

1 Feeding groundbait is as easy as loosefeeding and all it requires is a little practice to become perfect. The groundbait needs to be in position close to the angler so that it can be reached by hand.

2 The pole is moved to the forward position and the butt section is clamped between the knees and supported on the underside with the left hand. Should a fish take, the angler will strike with his left hand.

3 The right hand moves to the groundbait bowl and moulds a small nugget of groundbait into a ball. The groundbait needs to be formed just tight enough so that it will hold together when it is thrown.

4 The angler measures the distance the groundbait has to be thrown and as the float is usually fished just off the tip of the pole, the end of the pole acts as a marker. With practice great accuracy can be achieved.

5 To make sure of reaching the correct distance the angler takes up a standing position. The small nugget of groundbait is held in the palm of the right hand and is to be thrown forward underarm.

6 Once the angler is ready the groundbait is thrown upwards and outwards towards the pole tip. The tip of the pole may be slightly submerged when the throw is taking place, to help the angler to hold it. However, all the time that this action has been occurring, any movement of the float can still be struck with the left hand by flicking the pole upwards.

Catapult Bait Feeding

1 The angler wedges the bait catapult under his leg and fills it from the bowl with his left hand. The right hand controls the pole.

2 Lift the catapult with the left hand and guide it over to meet the right hand. Grasp the tag of the catapult with the right hand.

3 The pole is supported on the angler's leg by pressure of the arm and three fingers of the right hand. Thumb and forefinger hold the tag.

4 The catapult is extended with the left hand, and the loosefeed is aimed at the tip of the pole. When the angler lets go with his right hand the catapult shoots the feed forward. Although this may look a bit difficult to accomplish, with a little practice the angler can get the feed accurately over the tip of the pole every time. If at any time while feeding, the float is drawn under, the angler can always react instantly by pushing the pole up with his right hand to set the hook.

BELOW: Pole fishing beside a lock. Canal traffic may slow sport at times, but as boats are on these waterways, be alert.

Lure Fishing

A t one time or another all predatory fish can be taken on lures, and occasionally fish that are not normally predatory can also be taken. There are well-documented instances of carp, bream and barbel being caught on lures, and hooked in the mouth. Generally speaking, however, the coarse angler will be targeting pike and perch on lure fishing methods and, less frequently, zander and chub. The idea of a lure is to imitate the prey of a predatory fish, not necessarily in visual appearance but more in behaviour. Most predators react strongly to sudden movement and vibration, and these are the factors behind lure design and use.

ABOVE: The equipment required for lure fishing for pike-gathered on the bank.

Types of Lure Fishing

Modern lure fishing had its origins in a method that appears very neglected today: that of wobbling dead fish on special flights. Using freshly killed coarse fish with their swim bladders intact, simply attached by two trebles, and mounted so the tail is kinked, wobbled deadbaits are buoyant and lethally effective when drawn over shallows with heavy weed growth. The more disturbance they make the better, and the parallel with fishing a floating plug is obvious. You can mimic the diving plug by adding lead to the head of the fish. In fact, a method to try when deadbaiting for

pike in rivers, is to insert a short length of steel bar into the throat of the bait. This is then fished sink-and-draw style and the action is tremendous, especially against a current. As the fish is drawn towards you, it appears to swim quite normally, but slacken off and the bait dives. This is irresistible to pike.

Deadbait spinning was the forerunner of spinning with artificials, with the bait attached to special mounts equipped with vanes at the bait's head to make it revolve rapidly when drawn through the water. Fishing with lures can be exciting, especially in the warmer months

when the method is at its most productive. In particular, fishing with surface lures can be heart-stopping stuff, and it is an unforgettable sight to see a big pike launch itself from the depths and clear the water in an explosion of spray with your plug clamped firmly in its jaws.

Sub-surface lure fishing relies more on feel for timing the strike, but is no less exciting. When a spoon comes to a sudden juddering halt, to be followed by the vicious head shake as a pike turns away, or a light spinning rod buckles to the attentions of a big perch as it grabs a spinner, the experiences are not quickly forgotten.

ABOVE: A floating plug being drawn across the surface. As you always see the fish take when fishing a floating lure, you must let the fish turn with the lure before striking.

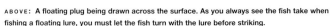

Pike wire

Three 30 lb (13.6 kg)
pike traces: 9 in
(23 cm), 12 in (30 cm)
and 18 in (45 cm)

Pike traces, singles
and doubles

Swivels and slim crimps

Tackle

You will not require a great deal of extra equipment for lure fishing. It depends on how much you plan to do.

Rods

If you are only intending to go on the occasional lure fishing trip, then you can certainly get away with the normal rods you would use for bait fishing. A light feeder rod will certainly be adequate for perch spinning, while a medium 10–11 ft (3–3.35 m) carp rod will handle any pike that swims. However, if you intend lure fishing to be a major part of your angling, it will reward you to invest in the right equipment. If you are going to be doing a lot of boat fishing, single-handed bait casting rods of around 9 ft (2.74 m) are ideal. The 9 ft (2.74 m) Spinflex, which can take main lines from 5–12 lb (2.27–5.44 kg), is a very versatile tool for the lure angler.

Reels

Regular lure casting and retrieval places great strain on reels, by wearing gears, loosening handles and weakening bail arm springs. For

OPPOSITE: Netting a pike. It helps to have a companion if you have to land a large fish.

efficient lure fishing, you also need very smooth line lay and long cast facilities, as well as a totally reliable clutch for when you eventually hook that monster. Aero GT reels have everything the lure angler needs. They are strong, light (most important when holding the rod constantly), and very smooth in operation with no bail arm backlash to create tangles. Most importantly, the better reels are vibration free, as continually retrieving a lure with a reel that is constantly wobbling is a tremendous irritation. Also important is the fighting drag system, an important safeguard when a very big fish intercepts your lure.

Lines and Trace Wires

Trace wire for lure fishing should be no less than 15 lb (6.8 kg), but this should be stepped up if you intend some big pike fishing at some of the large trout reservoirs. Where the pike are known to run to 40 lb (18.14 kg) you want traces of at least 25 lb (11.34 kg). Stainless seven strand trace wire, as well as being of very consistent quality, is thin and supple. This is important as it has minimum impact on lure action. As far as main lines are concerned, 12 lb (5.44 kg) is about right on most fisheries, but if

you are fishing very light spinners for perch you need to go lighter as you will find the action of the lure impaired. The frequent casting demands good abrasion resistance, and one of the best lines for this purpose is Sufix synergy.

Lure Fishing for Pike

Lure fishing for pike can be a thrilling experience, especially if you are fishing in clear water. If you wear a pair of polarized sunglasses you will be able to see the lure as it weaves its way back to the rod tip. A pike can often be seen following the lure and will strike it at the last possible moment, usually as the lure is being lifted to the surface of the water at the end of the retrieve. As the pike follows the lure, the excitement mounts and the angler's heartbeat races; when the pike strikes and is hooked, the speed and strength of the fight is frightening. In this sequence the angler is fishing fairly shallow water by a sluice, with a floating plug. This type of water is a well-known haunt for pike and every part of the water is covered systematically: the photographs tell the tale.

1 This angler is fishing with a floating plug. Although the plug is buoyant and floats, it is fitted with a vane under its chin, which will make it dive under the surface as it is being retrieved. The faster the angler retrieves the plug, the deeper it dives. The skilled angler can make the plug go up and down in the water to attract the interest of the pike.

2 Having picked a target area to cast towards, the cast is made. When fishing with any form of lure, it is common practice to search out all of the water you have in front of you. Start fishing to your left and then slowly fish around in an arc, covering every part of the water.

3 Once the plug hits the water in the centre of the swim, the bale arm on the reel is closed. The retrieve can now begin, and you should vary the speed. Slow, jerky movements will catch the eye of a roaming pike and it will quickly move in to investigate.

4 Keep watching the water for signs of a following pike, and keep a tight hold on the rod as a pike could strike the lure at any point of the retrieve. By wearing polarized glasses you will be able to see right down into the depths of the water and watch for the lure as it approaches.

5 As the lure approaches the rod tip, slow the retrieve down. If a pike has followed the lure this is usually the time it will strike as they like a slow-moving target. Very often the take will occur just as you are lifting the lure from the water.

6 A pike has taken the lure and the fight between the angler and pike is in full swing. The angler kneels on the bank to bring the pike under better control. This pike took the lure just as it was being lifted from the water at the end of the retrieve.

7 The pike is tiring and has been brought under control by the angler. This fish has not been deeply hooked and the treble of the floating plug can clearly be seen in the side of the pike's mouth.

8 The pike is landed safely and the angler shows the correct way to hold the fish with his fingers in the "V" shape under the pike's jaw. The thumb is then clamped against the outer jaw to hold the pike firmly. Pike can be landed in this way even if you have no net. But take great care not to get your fingers in the pike's mouth.

9 Use a mat while removing the hooks. Turn the pike on its back and use a pair of long-nosed forceps. Hold the jaws open by inserting two fingers under the gill cover on the underside of the jaw. The thumb is pressed on the lower jaw to force the jaws open. No damage can come to the fish and it can be returned to the water safely.

Fishing with Plugs

Plugs are wooden, plastic or metal lures designed to imitate the prey of predatory fish. There are now four basic types of plugs: floating divers, floaters, slow sinkers and suspenders. It is important to match the lure to the quarry and take note of the conditions, too.

Floating Diver Plugs

An old, established and well-known example of a floating diver plug is the Big S, which comes in a wide range of sizes. These lures carry a diving vane on the front, creating the dive effect when they are wound in: the faster the retrieve the deeper the dive. By altering the vane angle, the steepness of dive can be controlled. A small, steeply angled lip on the plug indicates that it is a shallow diver, and a deep-running bait will have a quite shallow-angled lip. A useful feature of this type of plug is that once you have submerged it with a sharp pull, say to 2 ft (60 cm) below the surface, a steady, constant retrieve will keep it at that depth, which is very useful for searching shallow, weedy areas.

Plugs with the ability to run at a set level at a controlled speed are the ones to select when you are searching a large water by trolling – towing the lure behind a slow-moving boat. Many plugs are now made in hollow plastic, and the body cavity filled with multi-reflective surfaces to mimic silver fish

scales. They are also filled with ball bearings so that they rattle, increasing the sound attraction. A further refinement in the floating diver category is jointed plugs, which have two body sections that can move independently, increasing even further the action and disturbance as they are brought through the water.

The Rapala is one of a family known as minnow plugs, which are all successful lures. Drifting a floating minnow plug downstream can help you fish at a further distance than you could probably cast with a light lure. Probably the best known is the Devon minnow, which is a finned, revolving variant well loved by salmon anglers.

Floating Plugs

All kinds of weird and wonderful designs are available, to imitate almost every animal, insect or reptile. Some of these are ideal for chub fishing as well as for pike. With these surface lures, a very erratic retrieve – stopping and starting in a jerky fashion to make them pop on to the water – can produce spectacular takes.

Another exciting surface presentation that produces vicious attacks is possible with an adaptation of the standard surface plug, which includes a small propeller at the front end, so that it actually buzzes when pulled at a high speed through the surface film. These are, appropriately enough, called propbaits. It is better to

tie these lures directly on to the line or trace with an open-looped knot without using snaps or swivels. When fishing with these, and in fact all surface lures, always keep your striking arm in check for a vital second or two. It is very easy to strike instantly in the excitement of the moment and pull the lure straight out of the fish's mouth. Just like the take of a chub on floating crust, let the pike turn with the bait before setting the hooks. Bear in mind that many lures have hook points that are far too blunt and it will pay to spend time sharpening them before fishing, especially when piking.

Diving Plugs

These are probably the least used, and reserved for those occasions when fishing a water of very variable depth with some deep holes to explore. They can be sub-divided into slow divers, like the Kwikfish, and fast divers like the Hi-Lo, which actually has an adjustable diving vane to vary its rate of descent. With divers, the technique is to count a set number of seconds after the plug hits the water before starting a steady retrieve, altering the delay periodically to vary the retrieve depth. Once at the required depth, increasing retrieve speed will send the lure deeper.

Suspending Plugs

These are interesting to use, the general idea being that they are of neutral buoyancy, and just hang "suspended" in the water when you stop retrieving for a moment. Restarting the retrieve makes them dive. This stop-and-go retrieve technique is effective for all species, but is apparently the most efficient way of lure fishing for zander, which are ultra-suspicious predators. When fishing for zander in this way, some of the takes to suspender plugs are vicious in the extreme and at high speed, so do not have your clutch setting too tight.

As fish see surface lures in silhouette, they often miss at the first attempt because of light refraction. Give them a chance to catch up with the lure and have another go. Anglers often mistakenly feel that the pike has deliberately "come short" at the lure when, in fact, it has genuinely missed its target and ends up just as frustrated as the angler.

A selection of popper lures

Plugs for salmon

A selection of deep floating diver plugs, shallow diving plugs and a jointed floating diver plug

Black-and-silver minnow plug

Fishing with Spinners and Spoons

The secret of successful spinning is speed and variation of retrieve. The perfect presentation is a nice, slow, controlled retrieve, occasionally flipping the lure to one side to cause additional vibration. Spinners are so called because at least part of the lure revolves. They attract fish by visual stimulus and create vibrations that act on the fish's lateral lines; if used correctly, they are sure to appeal to most predatory fish.

Many spinners are a little too heavy to allow a slow enough retrieve, especially in shallow water and, although a fast-moving lure will occasionally work, it is usually better to elect a lightweight spinner with an aluminium revolving blade. One of the best all-round spinners is the Rublex Ondex, available in various sizes and weights, closely followed by the Mepps Black Fury. Choose the Mepps in the deeper waters as, being slightly heavier than the Ondex, it requires a slightly faster retrieve in shallow water.

Swivel spinners

Spinning for Pike

When starting a spinning session for pike, always search first of all those areas where the pike are most likely to be, close to cover or ambush points, reedy margins, lily beds and drop-offs at the edges of gravel bars. In rivers, the same rules apply but, like stalking chub, always work upstream if spinning. Another tip is to start operations with the smallest spinner you have. Even big pike have been put down by big heavy lures, particularly in intimate little areas.

Spinning for Perch

This is one of the most effective methods of taking perch, especially in the large stillwaters, and if you know there are only jack pike present you can safely drop the trace strength to around 8 lb (3.63 kg) to achieve a better presentation. Perch rely more on visual stimulus to attack lures than pike, which react to sound vibrations, and flashing spinner blades imitate shoals of small fish turning in the water. This also explains why tasselled spinners are so effective. A red tassel imitates the tail of a roach or rudd.

In coloured water, in which perch feed avidly, more flashy lures will be needed, and it then pays to increase the size of the lure to make it more visible. In these conditions, choose one that gives good colour contrast.

Lures for pike and perch

Spinners should be retrieved as slowly as possible when fishing for perch, with occasional short bursts of speed to vary the presentation. In the event of the fish coming short, or hitting the lure without taking it, baiting the hooks with lobworms often makes a difference.

If you wish to spin very deep waters, heavier lures are among the best. These are designed to be bounced along close to the bottom, so should not be your choice in heavily snagged waters as it could prove expensive on tackle.

Spinning for Other Species

As well as for pike and perch, spinning can also be an effective method for taking chub. The same applies to zander in coloured water, where these lightweight spinners are best fished very slowly. Also effective for zander are fish-shaped spoons.

Chub can also be tackled with fly spinners, which are tiny spinners with the hook dressed as an artificial fly. This provides the very effective combination of the insect imitation with the flash of the spinning blade. Similar are fly spoons, which are tiny spoons with a dressed hook attached. The lightest lures of this family are designed to float or fish just below the surface, where, in combination with

Brightly coloured spinners

their mini blades or spoons, they make very effective hybrid lures.

These little lures are good for fishing over very snaggy areas and can be fished "dapping" by lowering them on to the water under trees, leaving them to float for a minute or two and then giving them a quick buzz across the water surface.

It is a common misconception that the only lures that can be used on the surface are plugs, when in fact lightweight spinners and spoons, as well as the more specialized spinner baits and hybrid lures, can all be fished on top very effectively. A spinner bait is a combination of a spinning blade and a skirted jig bait, which looks a bit weird but is a very effective lure in the upper layers of water. A hybrid lure could be a spinner-spoon, which is similar to the spinner bait but with a spoon blade replacing the jig bait. The effectiveness of all these lures on top is the splash they create on touch down and then the wake they leave behind them, which provokes some dramatic responses from pike.

Generally, the shape and thickness of the blade affects the action of the lure. A broad blade is ideal for stillwaters and slow streams, but it will rise to the surface. Thin blades have less resistance and can be fished in fast water without skating on the water surface.

Jerk bait

Reading the Water

efore you can catch fish you must fish where they are, but most anglers still select river swims with their own comfort in mind, rather than giving thought as to whether the swim actually contains the fish they are seeking. For consistent success in all aspects of river angling, you must develop ways of reliably locating your quarry.

ABOVE: The margins of lakes around the shores and reed beds are always likely spots to try for many species.

The Summer River

Even if you only fish rivers in the winter, time spent investigating the river in summer is never wasted. When the water is low and clear, and the weed beds and bankside vegetation at their height, river features are at their most obvious. Logging their position now is invaluable later in the season when the banks are barer and the river high and murky. Also, of course, the various species of fish are more easily seen in summer, and their feeding areas will always be a good starting point in winter.

Features to look for include smooth gravelly shallows, lily beds, undercut banks, positions of all rush beds, depressions in the river bed, underwater snags, deep runs under overgrown banks and so on. All these features will be attractive to one or more species of fish. Dace, roach and grayling will colonize the fast gravel, as will barbel, particularly at night. Big perch have an affinity for undercut banks and sedate, deep

marginal flows. Chub, barbel and big roach will often be found in depressions, while river bream and tench like nothing better than browsing through lily beds. Marginal rushes are favourite ambush points for pike, while the angler seeking specimen barbel and chub need look no further than the underwater snag.

Any area of smooth flow overhung by trees will be a banker in winter for many species, especially if the river rises sufficiently to form rafts of flotsam around the lower branches. Many of these features will be obvious by eye, but, if the river is shallow enough, you can wade through it. This is the fastest way to discover the variations in the bottom contours. If you are not comfortable doing that, or the river is too deep, take the trouble to plumb all the areas where the bottom is not visible, and make a careful note of the results.

There are many anglers who only fish rivers in the winter months, when much of the fishing is undoubtedly at its peak, and they base

their fish location on previous experience of the river plus their ability to read the water. Only stretches of river with character and variation in flow can be read accurately, and these will generally be of small to medium size. Straight, evenly flowing stretches, possibly wide and deep, present different location problems. You will discover, locating fish in these is often a painstaking process of elimination.

The Winter River

Swims that are good in summer will be equally reliable in winter, unless river conditions force the fish to move out. When higher, faster flows force them to move, they only move as far as they need to in order to find a comfortable station. This is where the ability to read the flow variations of a winter river is crucial to determining where the fish will relocate.

Examining the set of the various flows of a river at winter level soon confirms that what at first glance may appear unvarying current speed and direction from bank to bank is actually anything but uniform. There are usually numerous variations in the current, with regular divisions between fast and slower water, some of which are very pronounced. Such divisions between fast and slower flows are known as creases, and they are among the most reliable of all winter swims for many species.

LEFT: In a small stream, clear, shallow water and sparkling gravel enable you to check the depths of the river without trouble. They are also ideal conditions for spotting fish.

The Water Surface

Whatever the speed of flow, the water surface itself gives us vital clues to the sub-surface contours and vegetation. Certain areas run smoothly, while others are constantly or intermittently turbulent. Whether it be a gentle ripple or a substantial boil, such surface disturbance is a reflection of underwater irregularities. A constant boil or vortex is caused either by the shelving up of the river bed or by a large obstruction, such as an old tree stump. A shelving river bed is often accompanied by a diversion of flow if the bottom gravel slopes across river, and such a feature is a natural food trap, attractive to all species. But this is only true where the surface flow is relatively smooth away from the actual feature. If the current is fierce enough to result in heavily broken, boiling water, fish will vacate the area.

Constantly boiling water, caused by large irregular bottom debris, is rarely worth a second look. The whirlpools caused by such obstructions make it very uncomfortable for fish to cope with the constantly changing currents. One exception might be an area of very localized boiling, created where a large boulder or something similar rests on otherwise smooth gravel. Such a feature often causes a depression on the downstream side hollowed out by the current, and that creates a food trap. Such swims are most effectively fished upstream.

It is important to differentiate between heavily broken water caused by large debris, and the moderate constant ripple of shallows. The surface of shallow water will ripple even if the bottom is quite fine gravel containing small stones, and such areas only become unfishable when heavy flood water creates unacceptable levels of turbulence.

Depressions

These hollows in the river bed in extensive shallows are excellent holding areas, especially for chub, roach and barbel; look for smooth bits of surface amongst the ripple. Even a small depression is an important swim to locate, particularly if it is located in a long stretch of shallow water, when it may be the only natural holding spot in that section of river, particularly in high water. It is quite amazing how many big fish can pack into a tiny depression.

The Winter River – The Effect of Aquatic Vegetation

Intermittent undulations on the water surface betray the presence of sunken weed beds. Submerged rushes cause variable surface ripple, but of a different type from that over shallows, in that it is much more broken and, at normal height at least, the odd rush stem breaks the surface. An underwater rush bed also splits the flow, creating two types of swim. As the roots hold back the central water, a lee of slacker water forms downstream, before the two separated flows rejoin. Such slacks are very reliable swims, especially for chub, barbel and pike. Current diversion across river will create creases alongside the submerged rushes.

Ranunculus, or streamer weed, gives great variation of surface activity, as the long tresses undulate

TOP: Steady runs behind beds of rushes in mid river are likely to prove reliable swims for many species. Experience will teach you the likely places that are worth exploring.

ABOVE: Trees on the far bank are popular holding places. They are particularly loved by chub who feed on insects from the trees.

up and down in the flow. The water will run smoothly for a while, followed by a boil as the weed rises to just under the surface. This type of boil is short lived and subsides quickly.

Fishing in Streamer Weed

A deadly method of fishing in streamer weed is to place a bait right under the trailing fronds, by casting upstream and across from the boil, so that the bait alights on clean gravel beyond the root. The bait will then be settled naturally under the weed by

current action. The faster the flow, and the deeper the water, the further upstream of the boil you will need to cast to allow for the current speed. There is no doubt that interpreting the flows created by beds of streamer weed, particularly in high water, gives anglers the greatest difficulty.

However, as some of our finest fisheries have long stretches adorned with ranunculus, it is vitally important to know how to go about it. Initially, spend a few minutes just looking and making mental notes of the various surface characteristics. You will see many places where the water boils and then flattens, as the tresses wash up and down in the flow. But most important are those narrow areas of surface which run smoothly, without any boils or vortices. These indicate smooth gravel runs between streamer beds. A correctly presented bait on this gravel will slowly roll

round and settle under the adjacent streamer fronds. If there is a fish there this nearly always produces a take.

The Winter River – Crease Swims
Excellent swims are where the main current suddenly diverts across river. Shelving gravel banks create such swims, and where the current is steady this makes a hot spot. Food items drifting downstream are diverted across river by the shelf in a fairly narrow band, and fish are quick to take advantage of the easy pickings. The secondary consequence of this diversion is that it creates quite a sharp demarcation between the fast main current and the more sedate water that does not deviate across river. In higher, faster water, when fish are unwilling to fight the main flow, they will shift position on to the crease, or move to the slower water away from the demarcation line.

ABOVE: **Barbel fishing during a winter flood. High, coloured water in winter is a good place for barbel, and also other species, such as roach. Success in these conditions, especially if the day is relatively mild, is almost guaranteed.**

All junctions between fast and slow water can be considered crease swims, and their causes are many. A section of protruding bank, an old tree stump, a feeder stream ingress, a bend in the river, and a marginal weed bed can all lead to a diversion of the main flow and therefore a crease swim. Under normal conditions, the junction between the two flows is the most reliable area to fish.

If there is one rule of thumb with winter river angling, it is to locate an area of evenly paced flow and oily, smooth surface, of whatever depth. There is an excellent chance you will have located fish of many species.

LEFT: High coloured water and a bright winter's day with a mild southerly wind to "blow the hook to the fish's mouth". These conditions are virtually perfect and dreamed of by many anglers. In this type of water the angler may well record an exceptional bag of roach, as well as many other species.

BELOW: A featureless stretch of river in the Midlands. The slower and wider a river becomes, the more difficult it becomes to read – this is very true of the bottom reaches of large rivers such as the River Severn, for example. Often it will take an angler a number of years to work out the hot spots on any stretch, and in these cases it is essential to examine the river when there is a severe drought in summer. Low water reveals all the hidden snags and holes that will harbour fish.

The Winter River – Assessing More Featureless Stretches

Even on rivers that are mainly fast and shallow, with lots of character, there will be stretches which are deeper than average, sluggish, dead straight and virtually featureless. Although much less interesting, such sections can harbour some of the biggest fish on the river. The lower beats of many of our rivers are also more difficult to read the slower and wider they become. The lower reaches of the Severn and the Great Ouse are cases in point.

Where there is a distinct lack of features, it is even more important to locate those that are present, as they could attract very high concentrations of fish. On the Severn, for instance, sunken snags are magnets for barbel.

Any feature on a largely featureless stretch could be extremely significant and is well worth investigating. For example, an insignificant trickle from a rivulet or land drain will often attract roach, and a tangle of fallen branches may be colonized by big perch. Marginal bushes are important, even when they do not actually overhang the water. This is because the foliage ensures less bankside disturbance at that point, and bush root systems, especially hawthorn and blackthorn, often lead to undercutting the bank. Undercuts provide quiet refuges for fish on all stretches, but on a stretch with a lack of other features, they assume much greater significance.

Before starting to fish a uniform stretch, it is worth spending some time plumbing, to see whether underwater irregularities, such as depressions, exist. Also, unsuspected snags or sunken weed beds may manifest themselves. Even a small dip in the river bed could create a hot spot, as could an area of gravel in an otherwise muddy bottom.

Although it is sensible to devote time to any feature that is present, much of the fishing in fairly bland stretches of river will be a matter of painstaking elimination, or trusting to luck. Obviously, the latter is not an option if consistent success is your objective. If you are faced with a perfectly uniform stretch with no discernible variations of any type, there is no way of knowing exactly where the fish will be. You have to find them either by trial and error or by creating artificial hot spots and hoping the fish will come to you.

BELOW: A good chub taken in midwinter with snow on the ground. This fish was taken from a depression in midstream.

Stillwaters

Stillwaters present more of a problem than rivers. They all have distinctive taking places but often these are less apparent. Small stillwaters can be learned fairly quickly; vast trout lakes and reservoirs take much longer.

Understanding Estate Lakes

Estate lakes usually have bottom compositions of mud or silt and are frequently very weedy indeed. Bulrushes, reeds and water lilies are particularly common and these are favoured feeding sites of most species, and excellent ambush points for predators. The winter pike angler should make careful note of water lily beds. In the winter, roach love to feed among the dead roots which provide perfect camouflage for a hungry pike.

The essential difference between an estate lake and a gravel pit is that most such waters have much more even bottom contours. There will, however, be interesting features on most waters, generally caused by natural land undulations. The even bottom contours and rich feeding sites make many species much less nomadic than they are in gravel pits. Roach and bream shoals, for instance, can take up permanent residence in certain areas and their feeding times in these swims can be very predictable. Bream often travel around on well-defined patrol routes.

Many estate lakes, particularly the more naturally occurring or heavily wooded pond types, exhibit deep marginal areas, possibly as a result of land faults having created the water in the first place. Such marginal deeps, often overhung with foliage and possibly containing bottom debris of fallen timber, are a haven for pike and perch, as they attract hordes of fry. Carp also are fond of them.

One last general observation about estate lakes is that, because they are very often fairly small and enclosed, the effects of wind on where the fish are is less significant than on larger, more open waters. The only possible exception are carp, which are probably more affected by wind than other species. Even on smaller lakes, there is evidence that carp migrate to the windward bank in a steady wind.

An obvious location aid is seeing the fish themselves, and here estate lake fish are very obliging. Shallow water roach in rich lakes have the helpful habit of rolling regularly at dawn and dusk, as well as through the dark hours, and rudd regularly prime at the surface. Rudd is one of the more nomadic fish and on a large water binoculars are a boon to follow their dorsal fins breaking the surface.

Carp also show themselves readily, by rolling, head and tailing or swirling at the surface. They also betray their presence by bow waving – where a wake follows a carp swimming close under the surface; tenting – where a mound appears by magic in surface weed as the carp's back pushes upwards; and smoke screening – where large clouds of disturbed silt colour localized areas. Another common phenomenon is the sight of a faint "V", as the merest tip of the carp's dorsal cuts the surface film as it swims. To find estate lake tench, look no further than the margins. Hard against marginal rushes or lilies is a reliable swim, but the most reliable way of finding tench is to be there at dawn and watch for the characteristic frothy patches of "needle bubbles".

Location of pike in estate lakes, as in all waters, is obviously governed by the location of the prey fish, and they will therefore be found in the vicinity of any feature. Edges of rush beds or where rushes protrude out into the lake are good. Such rush headlands are popular ambush points.

Bays and inlets are used by perch shoals as traps in which to herd fry. Of all estate lakes, the one that seems to have the greatest affinity for big perch is the small but deep farm pond – the kind of water that appears to contain shoals of stunted rudd and crucians, but little else. When fishing these deep ponds for big perch, any area of underwater snags will be favoured, as will bankside root formations and overhanging foliage.

LEFT: The angler has cast a deadbait to a gravel bar in the middle of the gravel pit. Here he is setting a bite indicator.

Mapping Gravel Pits

The important features to locate on pits are the bars, gullies, gravel plateaux, sudden drop-offs and weedbeds. You need to know the bottom composition and the nature of bottom weed, especially if there are areas which are weed-free amongst otherwise densely weeded areas. These are important for the bream or pike angler. Bream, for instance, like to feed over areas that are naturally weed-free, while tench will happily browse amongst dense weed.

Some of these features can be indicated by visual evidence taken from the surrounding land. For instance, a gently sloping marginal area will indicate a similar gradient running out into the pit, while a steep shelf may indicate a deep marginal trench. Perhaps the most important evidence is a prominent point, or a spit of land protruding into the pit. This usually indicates the presence of an underwater gravel bar, a feature attractive to all gravel pit species.

Other visual evidence can be gleaned from the activities of water birds, particularly swans, coots and grebes. Swans can only feed on bottom weed that they can reach,

LEFT: The angler has cast a deadbait to a gravel bar in the middle of the gravel pit. Here he is setting a bite indicator.

OPPOSITE: Water lilies growing at the edge of a small lake. Carp and tench find them particularly attractive.

RIGHT: The feeder stream of a large reservoir in a very dry summer. A gully like this will always hold good fish when filled.

while coots are great feeders on bottom weed, but do not like to feed too deeply. If coots are continually diving in one spot, you may have discovered an important gravel plateau. The pike or perch angler can do a lot worse than study the activities of great crested grebes, as they will continually dive where hordes of fry are to be found.

Finding the sub-surface features of a pit can be a long and laborious process, and mapping is far simpler if you have access to a boat, especially if it is coupled with an echo sounder. If you have no boat, mapping a gravel pit with standard plumbing methods is very efficient if you know what you

are doing. Set up a large, easily visible sliding pike float with a 2 oz (50 g) lead. Set the float shallow, say about 4 ft (1.22 m), and cast it out to maximum fishing range to the left-hand extremity of the swim, aiming at an easily identifiable point on the horizon. If the float lands in water deeper than this, it will obviously sink like a stone. Then begin a slow retrieve, reeling in about 6 ft (1.83 m) of line at a time before allowing out a little slack to let the sliding float work properly. If the lead has moved on to a feature shallower than 4 ft (1.22 m), the float will pop up to the surface. By covering the swim this way, at progressively greater depth settings, you can soon discover the location and extent of all features in the water in front of you.

On the day of fishing you may need a permanent marker, and this is simple to achieve. Having identified the feature, cut the line about 12 in (30 cm) above the sliding float stop knot. Form a loop in the line and form another loop in the reel line. Tie both loops tightly together with PVA and cast out to the required spot. After a few minutes, retrieve the main line, leaving the marker in place with no trailing line that might foul the line when you are fishing. At the end of the day, use a grapple lead with treble hook attached to retrieve these markers from the water.

Understanding Reservoirs

Reservoirs fall into two types: those created by damming natural valleys, so that their feeder streams backfill the valley to the limits dictated by the dam and the land contours, and those more artificially formed by creating huge bowls supported by earthworks.

Some of our best stillwater coarse fishing is to be found on water supply reservoirs, and it is essential to devote time to determining the underwater contours if you are going to get the best out of them. Bowl-type reservoirs are usually of fairly consistent depth, although they will normally get shallower towards one end. Any sudden depth variation in a reservoir of this type will be rare, and if one exists it will always be worth concentrating on.

Naturally-flooded valleys provide far more interesting fishing. The original stream or streams that drain into the valley are the most important features to locate, as they will be deeper, with hard gravel beds, while the surrounding land could be mud. They will have a natural current, against which fish like to swim, and will be the first areas to show the ingress of coloured water when it rains and high water swells the feeder streams. A simple way to pinpoint the route of a stream bed is to visit the reservoir the day after heavy rain, particularly if you can gain a high vantage point. You will often see coloured water snaking along the path of the stream bed. It needs, however, to be calm. If there is a wind and the

water is rough, rapid mixing occurs and the browner fresh water quickly becomes general.

The land surrounding a reservoir gives accurate clues as to the marginal bottom contours. A section of steep bank, therefore, will indicate similarly steeply increasing marginal water depth. Conversely, long fingers of water are likely to be shallow and gently shelving, and these are places where the angler can expect to find shoal fish, such as perch and roach, when they are present.

Having made note of all the visual clues you must then fill in the gaps with the more painstaking manual mapping, although there will usually be less dramatic depth variations in reservoirs than in natural lakes.

ABOVE: Queenford Lagoon. This water is badly affected by the prevailing wind.

The Effects of Wind and Weather on Stillwaters

Carp, rudd and bream are the first fish to be influenced by strong winds, usually migrating to the windward shores. On reservoirs and lakes, a favourable wind is one off the dam and pushing towards the shallows. These fish love to feed along the windward slopes of gravel bars in pits and similarly, they love to browse on the rising ground towards lake shallows. Tench also feed avidly on shallows in rough conditions, but it is the rough conditions that stimulate their feeding rather than their following of the wind.

Roach also respond to strong wind, although it is the secondary effects of the wind that are important, such as the sub-currents that are created in stream-fed reservoirs. If these streams are swollen with rain, the increased flows, combined with the effects of wind, create all manner of complex sub-flows, known as undertows. Find a good undertow, at or near a stream bed, in coloured water, and roach will not be far away. For the predatory species, the prevailing weather and water conditions will affect their location only in as much as it affects the movements of the prey fish.

LEFT: A man-made reservoir. The land around slopes gently down to the water and the margins are relatively shallow. The prevailing wind blows across the water to the north-east shore.

Fishing in Europe

Many of our coarse fish, principally roach, tench, bream, barbel and zander, are found in many parts of Europe, particularly France, Germany, Holland and Belgium, but it is fair to say that the main interest of British anglers travelling abroad for coarse fish will be in pursuing big catfish, carp or pike.

ABOVE: **A giant catfish caught in France.**

Catfish

Closest to home is France, and the rivers Saône and Loire have both produced catfish in excess of 100 lb (45.4 kg). On the River Saône the best fishing is the 100 miles (161 km) or so stretching from Lyon to Chalon. The Loire is productive between Decize and Gien. As well as these two rivers, one or two lakes in France hold big catfish, notably Lake Cassien which produced a monstrous fish estimated at well over 100 lb (45.4 kg) a few years ago.

Another European river holding huge cats to over 300 lb (136 kg) is the River Danube, which runs through Germany, Austria, the Czech Republic, Romania and Hungary. In all those countries the river has been fished successfully by British cat hunters. As far as stillwaters are concerned, most of the large Hungarian, Austrian and Swiss lakes hold big catfish, and one

of the most famous fisheries in the former Yugoslavia for catfish is the huge Vransko lake.

The two countries most of interest to British anglers who want organized catfishing are Germany and Spain. Most of the lakes in southern Germany hold cats, the most famous day-ticket fishery being Schnackensee, near Nuremberg. In Spain, it is the mighty River Ebro that has produced dozens of enormous cats, some weighing well over 100 lb (45.4 kg), for visiting anglers.

For those seeking that real leviathan however, eastern Europe now holds the allure, and the Rivers Desna and Volga of Russia regularly produce cats over a staggering 400 lb (181 kg). Before you go abroad on a catfish expedition make sure you obtain the correct, up-to-the-minute information, especially if you intend visits to politically sensitive regions.

ABOVE: **A beautifully streamlined carp caught in France.**

Carp

By far the greatest numbers of British anglers travelling abroad are going in search of the very big carp that are available. Probably the most famous venues are in France, with Lake Cassien leading the way. Other famous waters include Salagou and St Quoix. Most stillwaters in France contain carp, as do many of the rivers, the River Seine having produced some very big fish indeed.

As well as in France, big carp are to be found over a good part of the globe. There are big fish to be found in the lakes of most European countries, as well as in Canada, the United States, the Canary Islands, the Far East, Africa and Australia. The canal drainage systems of the Netherlands are reliable and are known to hold a good head of carp to large sizes.

The casual angler who wishes to fish for carp abroad, and be looked after, has good opportunities. The Carp Society should be contacted as it owns overseas carp waters where its members can fish.

Pike

Some of the biggest pike in Europe are found in the Scottish lochs, Irish loughs and the huge trout reservoirs of Wales and England. For this reason, few anglers seem to travel abroad in search of big pike. However, some of the big waters of Holland still offer excellent potential, while there are undoubtedly huge fish in other European countries. The problem is that in many European countries people eat their catch, and in Germany all fish are killed. As pike are one of the slower-growing fish, and react badly to pressure, they have suffered as a consequence. Around Great Britain we still have excellent pike fishing. Sweden, also has some huge pike – some weighing nearly 50 lb (22.7 kg) – have been taken from estuaries in the Baltic Sea. Swedish pike fishing is tightly controlled.

ABOVE: **A trio of huge Swedish pike.**

Tying Knots

The knots below illustrate a variety that are commonly used by coarse, sea and game anglers. Beginners should practise first with string since this is easier to handle than nylon.

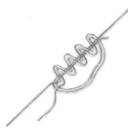

Mahseer Knot
This knot is well used among specimen anglers and in particular, those travelling abroad. As the name suggests, it was originally used by Mahseer anglers in the giant fast-flowing Indian rivers. A good all-round knot for tying hooks to line, swivels, or joining two lengths of line together.

Palomar Knot
This is a popular knot for many anglers, especially among carp anglers who often use this knot when tying hooks on to braid rather than nylon. The knot causes the minimum strangulation and is therefore kinder to lines, particularly braid lines which can part if too much friction is applied.

Four-turn Water Knot
The water knot is well used by coarse, sea and game anglers and offers a good, strong, reliable knot for joining two lengths of line together. In game fishing circles it is widely used for creating droppers when fishing a team of flies, while the coarse angler will often use it to create a paternoster link.

Five-turn Sliding Stop Knot
A stop knot can be created from heavier line or coloured power gum, to act as a marker when distance fishing. Its most common use, though, is as a stop when float fishing in deeper water. Tied on the line above the float at a set depth, it stops the float sliding any higher up the line.

Uni Knot
This knot is extremely versatile and has a good following among anglers who prefer to use braided mainlines. It is used by sea anglers where the tying of large hooks to heavy-duty line is required. It is also a good knot to use with standard mono lines and offers a great strength when used for tying on hooks.

Double or Full Blood Knot
Most commonly used for joining two lines together. A good knot for the coarse angler who needs a knot to join a lower breaking strain hooklength line to the mainline. As it is a strangulation knot it should be wetted before pulling down tight. This will help to prevent friction burns on the line.

Spade End Knot
Used mainly by the coarse angler, this knot is very useful for tying on spade end hooks. Although many continental anglers are able to tie tiny hooks like 24s by hand, there is in fact a gadget known as a hook tyer that will produce this knot for you in a fraction of the time it takes you to tie it.

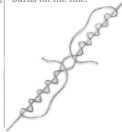

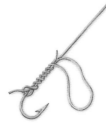

1 Start with a 360° degree circle in the line with the loose end pointing away from the bend of the hook. The hook should lie over the line.

2 Wind the outside of the loop over the hook shank about seven to eight times. Pull the ends to tighten, and the line will be whipped into place.

Shock Leader Knot

This knot has been specially developed to join a heavy leader to a lighter mainline. It is a much-used knot for the beach angler who is casting long distances. A length of heavier line, usually 50lb (22.68 kg) is joined to the mainline. This leader will then take the brunt of the cast and stop the lighter mainline from breaking.

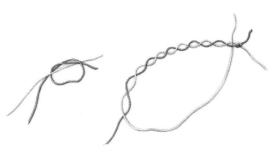

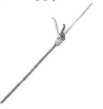

1 Tie an overhand knot in the heavier leader and pass the lighter line through the knot alongside the protruding gap.

2 Pull the overhand knot in the leader as tight as possible, then wrap the tag of the lighter main line around the leader a minimum of six times, but not more than ten. Next, thread the tag back through the first wrap formed, the one right up against the overhand knot.

3 Form the knot, first with gentle pressure on the mainline against the leader, then with equal pressure as the knot closes.

4 The finished knot should be pulled firmly to ensure the 'creep' has been taken up. The tag should be trimmed.

Double Overhand Loop

This simple but effective loop is most commonly used to accommodate a loop-to-loop hooklength. It can also be used to house a swivel or weight, by simply slipping the loop through and over the swivel or lead.

1 Form a loop at the end of your line.

2 Tie an overhand knot with the loop.

Locked Half Blood Knot

This knot is used for tying on hooks or swivels to the line. It is a firm favourite among sea and coarse anglers for the joining of eyed hooks. Sea anglers often use this for tying down swivels. Being a sort of strangulation knot, it needs wetting with saliva before being tightened down, to prevent friction burn.

1 Thread the line through the eye of the hook or swivel and twist the tag and mainline together. Complete three to six twists.

2 Thread the tag back through the first twist. The heavier the weight of the line, the fewer twists you will need to use.

3 Add another wrap to the knot.

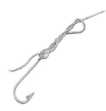

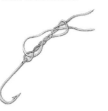

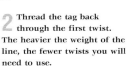

3 Pull the line, (but not too tightly) to begin with, so that the knot starts to form.

4 To lock the knot, thread the tag through the open loop which has formed at the top of the knot.

5 Pull the knot up firmly and test the knot to see that it holds. Trim off the surplus tag.

4 Close up the knot tightly and the loop is ready. This knot is also used when joining a cast to a mainline.

Grinner Knot

This knot is used by many anglers to attach the fly to the leader. It is very secure, and with practice it is easy to tie. There are several knots used by anglers to do this, Tucked Half Blood Knot, Turle Knot and Double Turle Knot being some of them.

1 Take the line through the eye of the hook, take it over the line and then make an overhand knot.

2 Add three or four turns to this overhand knot, depending on the thickness of the line you are using.

3 Pull both ends to tighten the knot, moistening it with saliva to prevent any line burn.

Loop Knot

This is a similar knot to the Grinner, and the first stages of tying the knot are the same. However, once the first overhand knot has been tied the turns are added around the mainline. This makes a good strong knot, but it is not quite as neat as some others.

1 Take the line through the hook and then tie an overhand knot.

2 Take three or four turns around the mainline above the overhand knot.

3 Pull both ends of the line to tighten the knot securely in place.

Surgeon's Knot

This is a good knot when you have to use to join two lengths of line of different strengths. It is used by sea anglers when joining a shock tippet to a main line. The only problem with this knot is that it can be difficult to tighten properly.

1 Lay the ends of the two lines to be joined side by side. Make sure you have allowed enough line.

2 Make four overhand turns, carefully keeping the two lines as level as possible.

3 Pull steadily and slowly on all four ends to tighten the knot properly. This can be difficult.

The Needle Knot

Needle and Nail Knots are the best ways of attaching a leader to a fly line. Their main advantage is that they form a straight knotless link with the line that runs no risk of catching in the top ring of the rod. They also enable the angler to add a thick length of nylon to the fly line to assist in tapering the cast and presenting the fly more accurately to the fish. There are many versions of this knot, all of which are relatively easy to tie with practice. The version shown here is one of the simplest knots.

1 Heat a thin needle. Push the point of the needle up the core of the line.

2 Thread the nylon on the needle and push the needle out at the side.

3 Take the needle a short distance down the line and push it right through.

4 Pull the nylon through and then bring the needle back and repeat stage 3.

5 Make the second hole nearer the end of the line as shown. Thread the nylon through.

6 Tie a figure-of-eight knot at the end of the nylon to act as a stop and pull the knot tight.

Index

INDEX

Acknowledgements

The publisher wishes to thank the following individuals and suppliers for their help and the loan of equipment and materials for photography:

Dave Ellyatt
Drennan International Limited
Bocardo Court
Temple Road
Oxford OX4 2EX
Tel: (01865) 748989

Mike Ashpole
Ashpoles of Islington
15 Green Lanes
London N16 9BS
Tel: (020) 7226 6575

Mr Brian Frattel
Farlows
5 Pall Mall
London SW1Y 5NP
Tel: (020) 7839 2423

Martin Ford
27 Willesden Avenue
Walton
Peterborough PE4 6EA
Tel: (01733) 322497

Andrea Barnett
Hinders of Swindon
Manor Garden Centre
Cheney Manor
Swindon SN2 2QJ
Tel: (01793) 333900

Lyn Rees
Shimano (UK) Ltd
Felindre Fishery
Blaen-Nant-Ddu
Felindre
Swansea SA5 7ND
Tel: (01792) 796584

Fishing suppliers:

Lawrence Short
TraceAce Tackle Ltd
2 Cottall Avenue
Chatham
Kent ME4 6HG
Tel: (01634) 720720

Tony Caton
Gemini Tackle Co
Gemini Works
Mill Lane
Market Rasen
Lincolnshire LN7 6UA
Tel: (01472) 852966

Relum
Carlton Park Industrial Estate
Saxmundham
Suffolk
IP17 2NL
Tel: (01728) 603271

PICTURE CREDITS
The publisher would like to thank the following individuals for their kind permission to reproduce pictures in this book:

Martin Ford & Dave Barham pp. 12 b; 15 c; 33 c; 35 tr; 84 tr; 94 cl & r, bl & r; 100 tr; 103 tr; 104 bl; 105 tr; 107 b; 108 b.
Peter Gathercole p. 2; 26 b.
Graham Marsden pp. 17 tr; 72 br; 121.
Tony Miles pp. 8; 9; 10 b; 11; 14–15; 15 tr; 16 b; 17 b; 18 b; 19; 23 tr & b; 25 t; 28 b; 32 bl & br; 33 t; 34 b; 35 tl & cl; 36 b; 37; 40 c; 43 tl & br; 61 br; 62 br; 65 br; 68 tl; 72 br; 80 bl; 81 bl; 84 t & c; 85 b; 86 b; 89 cr; 90 tr; 96 b; 98; 99; 109 t; 114 bl; 115; 116; 117; 118; 119; 120.
John Wilson pp. 1; 4–5; 6–7; 13; 20 c & b; 21 t & b; 22 b; 23 tl; 24 b; 25 c; 29 tl & c; 30 bl; 31; 38 b; 39; 40 tr; 41 tc & br; 44 br; 46 c; 47 cr; 48 tr; 49; 51 tl; 53 tr; 55; 89 t.

key: r = right, l = left, t = top, c = centre; b = bottom

Notes

NOTES

NOTES

NOTES